# THE ART
## *of* LIVING

# THE ART
## *of* LIVING

❖

## BOB PROCTOR
### *With* Sandra Gallagher

JEREMY P. TARCHER / PENGUIN
*an imprint of Penguin Random House*
*New York*

JEREMY P. TARCHER/PENGUIN
An imprint of Penguin Random House LLC
375 Hudson Street
New York, New York 10014

Most Tarcher/Penguin books are available at special quantity discounts for bulk purchase for sales promotions, premiums, fund-raising, and educational needs. Special books or book excerpts also can be created to fit specific needs. For details, write: SpecialMarkets@penguinrandomhouse.com.

ISBN 978-0-399-17519-0

Printed in the United States of America
1   3   5   7   9   10   8   6   4   2

*Book design by Gretchen Achilles*

# CONTENTS

# PREFACE

As far as I know, Bob Proctor is the only person who has been studying personal development every day for more than half a century. His work conveys the most valuable kind of information—how to get out of your own way so you can have a happy, healthy and massively wealthy life. He has done phenomenal work around the world, helping millions of people and countless organizations reach their biggest goals.

Bob is the last living teacher with a direct link to the great lineage of Andrew Carnegie, Napoleon Hill and Earl Nightingale. There is no one on the planet like this man and his life-transforming teachings. And he doesn't just teach it, he lives it! Bob is in his early eighties and he has more energy and enthusiasm for life than anyone I know. He acts like he is just getting started as his life's mission continues to be what it has been for the past fifty-plus years—to help as many people as possible master the art of living with no limits.

The most extraordinary aspect of Bob Proctor and his teachings is that he is a true conscious competent. In other words, he does extremely well, and he is consciously aware of why he does extremely well so he can share it with others in a way they can immediately put to use. It took him nine and a half years of serious searching, working with great mentors, teachers and books, to find out how and why his life changed. When he realized the truth of what had happened, all he wanted to do was teach it to others. To his amazement he found that almost all highly successful people are unable to articulate why they are so successful. They or their superiors satisfy themselves with the idea they are smart or have a good education or had good teachers. But there are a lot of smart people who had a great education and had smart teachers who are not doing well at all. When a person is highly successful in an endeavor and they cannot articulate why they are, they have something very powerful going for them that they are unable to give to another. Proctor is not only successful, he knows why he is and therefore he has the most valuable kind of information and it is transferable.

Bob Proctor truly believes we are all God's highest form of creation, that we have been blessed with magnificent mental faculties, and that the only thing missing is what wise King Solomon urged us to develop, and that is our understanding. We must understand who we are, why we are doing what we are doing and how to change what we are doing if we are not satisfied with our results. Proctor is a master at teaching just that.

I am grateful for the invaluable contribution he has made to my life. His teachings have empowered me to find my purpose and have the courage to pursue it. I feel incredibly privileged to be his friend, and I am so grateful to be his business partner at our company, the Proctor Gallagher Institute.

The lessons that you require to achieve any result you want are locked up between the covers of this book. What he shares is truly the art of living. As you turn the page imagine that you are walking right into one of Bob Proctor's classes.

—SANDRA GALLAGHER

# WHATEVER IT IS, YOU CAN GET IT

## *Reclaiming the Power of Your Mind*

was on a coaching call yesterday, and at one point I said, "You know, one hundred years from now, maybe even sooner than that, people are going to look back and consider what we do with children to be a criminal activity. They really will. It will *be a criminal activity!*"

Stop and think of the freedom a child has when he is small, just a little tiny baby. His imagination takes him wherever he wants to go. Children live in a phenomenal world where they can do anything they want. They can become pilots; they can be tightrope walkers; they can walk straight across Niagara Falls and have no problem at all. It's done right there in their marvelous mind.

Then we send kids to school and that fantastic creative process is suddenly a bad thing. The child's imagination is called "not paying attention." Drifting off into the glorious realm of the imagination for a few moments elicits a swift *"What are you doing?!"* from a teacher. It's a punishable offense! And those punishments are very effective. You beat a little kid up a couple of times for doing something and guess what? They'll stop doing it. So instead of being praised and encouraged to develop their imagination—an incredible mental faculty—they're made to virtually shut it down completely.

The late Stella Adler, a fantastic acting coach, said, "Grownups take the life out of things. It's better to make things up, to use the imagination, than to kill them." I couldn't agree more.

So now, here we are as adults, paying thousands of dollars, taking days off work or away from home, just to learn how to use our imagination again. But we have to. We have to all get back to a place of being able to access that phenomenal power because everything made by man that you see is nothing but the physical manifestation of somebody's imagination. That's what everything in your field of view inside this room right now is.

I used to have an office on Bayview Avenue in Toronto. We had a cleaning business where we cleaned offices. That's how I started washing floors. One day I thought, *We should get a car phone!* So we got a car phone and we put a supervisor on the road, and he would go around supervising all the cleaners, and I could get him on the phone. We had to mount ski racks on the top of his car to hold the aerial up so that we *might* be able to get him because there were only half a dozen channels on the phone and it didn't work very well. Today, of course, there are millions of lines open—millions. We all have one. And we can communicate with another person on their frequency. How did this happen? Someone imagined it, that's how.

If I took your picture right now, I could send it to anyone anywhere in the world. All I have to do is hit send and *bang!*, it is immediately 100 percent present in all places at the same time. If you were in São Paulo, you'd get the picture. If you were in San Francisco, you'd get the picture. If you were in Shanghai, you'd get the picture. If you were in Chicago, you'd get the picture. Why? Because the picture is everywhere. The only thing that makes it materialize is something that resonates with it: your number. *Boom!*, you've got it!

A thought is just the same as that picture. The only thing that stops a thought is that which resonates with the thought.

We can communicate telepathically with anyone, anywhere in the world, and we're doing it all the time. We just don't know what we're doing. Why? Because nobody taught us what we're doing, and so we grow up ignorant.

Think about this. When a little squirrel is born, nobody has to fend for it. That little squirrel runs up and down trees right away. It will look for nuts. It'll find something. It feeds itself. A little human baby, on the other hand, will die if you don't look after him or her. You see, the little squirrel operates by instinct, which is perfect. The squirrel is totally at home in its environment. We are totally disoriented in ours. Why? Because even though we've been given the mental faculty to create our own environment, we don't do it. Why don't we do it? Because we're told, "That's silly" . . . "Grow up!" . . . "That's not realistic!" . . . "Who do you think you are?" . . . all that jazz.

So here we've got human beings, with marvelous minds, and they're struggling, thinking they are stuck with the conditions or circumstances they're surrounded by. I'd like to do it but I can't because . . . Whatever follows "because" is the circumstance, and they become subservient to the circumstance. The circumstance becomes their version of God . . . and they do what their perception of the circumstance dictates. They don't even try to come up with a better way.

You're here to learn how to create multiple sources of income so that you can have financial freedom. Now I know you may be thinking, *Oh, I couldn't do that.* Why couldn't you do that? *Because I've never done that.* Can you imagine if you didn't learn to do things that you'd never done? You'd still be lying in your crib, playing with your toes. You would!

But you had to get up and put one foot in front of the other. You had to be taught to do that. They'd hold your hand—"He took a step on his own! Did you see that? He took a step on his own! He's walking! Oh, he just fell over. Oh, he's hurt himself!" You tottered, you stumbled, and it took you some time. But sure enough, you learned to walk.

Whatever "it" is, you *can* do it. You simply have to learn *how*.

I once read that the Wright brothers' father, who was a bishop in a reform church, told them they were going to burn in hell for suggesting they could fly; that if God had intended us to fly, we'd have wings.

Of course, that was believed for centuries. It was also believed that the world was flat. We really bought into it, we really believed it—and not that long ago! According to the prevailing wisdom of the time, how could the world possibly be round?! How would you live on the side?! Forget the bottom. And when you watched a ship disappear, it looked like it fell off! See, logic dictated that the world couldn't *possibly* be round, so that's what was believed.

Do you suppose that people were *thinking* when they bought into that idea? Do you think they were using their marvelous imagination when they insisted that we couldn't fly? I don't think so.

Earl Nightingale was a mentor of mine, and I learned

so much from him. I remember him saying, "If most people said what they were thinking, they would be speechless."

You'll find people competing with people. There's somebody they don't even like and they're competing. "I'm going to beat her!" What for? Why would you spend any time thinking of her? She's not even a nice person. Why would you spend *any* time thinking about that person? And if you're going to think about her, just see the good qualities in her. Because if you don't, you're putting yourself in a bad vibration.

A lot of people are nervous when meeting me. I find that amusing. I remember one time, years ago, I was working at a convention for Metropolitan Life in Toronto. There were many people at this convention. I saw this one guy—he would walk toward me and then he'd go away, walk toward me, go away. He was nervous about meeting me. It was fairly obvious.

Finally, his manager brought him over and said, "Bob,

I want you to meet Harry." The guy's hand was soaking wet. He was shaking. The manager said, "He's nervous meeting you." I started laughing, then I quickly said, "I'm not laughing at you, but if I said I was nervous meeting you, wouldn't you think that was funny? I mean, why would anyone be nervous meeting me? I know you think, *Why would anyone be nervous meeting me?* You'd think that. So do I."

Why would we do that? Why would we let another person's presence, a person we don't even *know*, intimidate us? Why would we feel like we are less than he or she is? Why would we shrink mentally? We have to be trained to do that. We weren't born with that.

But listen: We're big boys and girls now. We have the ability to *think*. So let's start thinking of what we really *want* to do. Let's get rid of the idea of what we have to do. You don't *have to do* anything. You'll say, "Well, you have to breathe." No, you could put a plastic bag over your head and finish it. You could. "Well, you *have* to pay taxes." No, you don't. You don't! You could go to jail or go to a tax-free zone. You don't have to pay taxes. You don't have to do anything.

You know what we've got to get straight in our head? We *choose* to do *everything* we do.

Viktor Frankl, the Viennese Jewish psychiatrist who was sent to a German concentration camp during the Second World War, wrote a book called *Man's Search for Meaning*. Quite a good book. In it, he said that regardless of the intellectual or psychological abuse he was subjected to in the camp, no one could cause him to think something he didn't want to think.

The same is true of your actions. We choose to do everything that we do. "She made me do it!" Oh no, no, no, no, no. She didn't make you do it. There might have been a little war if you'd decided not to do it. The alternative might have been uncomfortable. But she didn't make you do it—you chose to. We've got to take responsibility for what we're doing. We've got to take responsibility for our life!

❖

Here's the point: When you go to do something that you have never done, there are going to be all kinds of crazy things going on inside of you. There's going to be that little voice inside that talks to you and says, "Who do you think you are? You can't do that. You couldn't possibly be there at nine a.m.! You've got to be *here* at nine, you've got to do this." And that little voice inside frequently wins the conversation. It turns into a battle, and more often than not, that little voice inside wins it.

So when a person doesn't make the call, they don't ask anyone to buy the $100,000 policy. Then down the road they say, "Well, it wouldn't have worked, anyway. That's not going to make a difference. Some people can't afford that!"

Nonsense. People can afford whatever they want. If you go home and go through your house, you'll see it's full of stuff you don't need. You bought it because you *wanted* it. And when you really want something, you will always get whatever is required to have it . . . always. That is an absolute law of your being. When you make a decision, you flip your brain onto a different frequency. You begin to attract whatever is on that frequency. Now if you understand this, it makes everything a little easier. It makes it a lot better. If you don't understand it, it becomes fairly difficult. So we're going to try and understand it.

To do that I think it would be helpful for you to know where I come from. I want to share with you how this all started.

# DO EXACTLY WHAT I TELL YOU TO DO

## *The Infallible Recipe for Success*

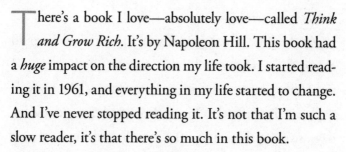

There's a book I love—absolutely love—called *Think and Grow Rich*. It's by Napoleon Hill. This book had a *huge* impact on the direction my life took. I started reading it in 1961, and everything in my life started to change. And I've never stopped reading it. It's not that I'm such a slow reader, it's that there's so much in this book.

How it came into my life is quite a story. All these years later, it still amazes me.

At the time, I was working for the East York Fire

Department, in the East York suburb of Toronto. It was the best job that I ever had, up to that point. I really shouldn't have been there. I should not have gotten that job. There were hundreds, maybe even a few thousand people who applied for that job. There's a certain element of society who all want to be firemen or police officers because firemen and police officers earn a little bit better than factory workers or waiters. I always thought being a fireman was better than being a police officer because we got to go to bed when we were on duty at night and the police officers couldn't.

Anyway, there was an advertisement in the newspaper—they were going to hire twenty-one firemen in East York. We had just moved to East York. I grew up in the Beaches area of Toronto, and I thought, *Wow, that would be something.*

At the time, I was working at a gas station. I would change tires, change oil, lubricate cars, wash cars . . . I was doing it for a dollar an hour, forty-eight hours a week, six days a week. One week a month I worked seven days, so I got three days off a month, and I was earning about $50 a week.

There was a magistrate who lived two doors up from my mother: Magistrate Lynn. I did not know him. I didn't know what the man looked like. But I knew he was a magistrate. So I went and knocked on his door, and I said, "You don't know me, sir, but my mother lives a couple doors from here. They're hiring firemen here in East York and I was going to put in an application, and I wonder if there's anything you could do to help me."

I think he was impressed that I asked him. "Oh," he said, "Come on in, son." He got on the phone, called the mayor and said, "I've got a young guy here who I'd sort of like to get on the fire department." And whoosh—I was on the fire department!

Now, you had to weigh 160 pounds. I had never weighed 160 pounds in my life. I was going to a gym, trying to put on weight, because I knew I had to have a physical. I was drinking *Weight On*—concentrated fat— attempting to gain weight, and I had to drink orange juice with it so I wouldn't gag. I was trying desperately to put weight on, but I still weighed 135 pounds!

So off I go for my physical in the township office and this old doctor said, "So you're going to be a fireman, are you, son?"

And I said, "Yes sir, yes sir."

He said, "Well, go over there and weigh yourself."

I got on the scale and he asked, "What's it say?"

I say, "160 pounds."

He stopped for a second and then he said, "Well, we'll leave it at that," and wrote it down. And there I was, on the fire department!

I worked seven days and seven nights a month. When you got on the night shift you'd go in the kitchen, make something to eat, maybe make a cup of tea, watch some TV, and when it got late, you'd make your bed and go to sleep. It was a real imposition if someone started a fire in the middle of the night and you had to get up and go put it out!

No one had *ever* quit that job. Not one person had quit since 1934. I'd go to sleep at night, get up in the morning from the firehouse, go and play golf. Go and shoot pool. I had doubled my income, and I hardly had to work! I was virtually retired. I thought I'd died and gone to heaven.

Then one day, I was sitting in the kitchen and a man who lived near the firehouse, whose name was Ray Stanford, came up and sat down with his cup of coffee. Ray was an incredible man who spent most of his time trying to wake people up.

Ray asked, "Bob, what would you rather be doing?"

I said, "I wouldn't rather be doing anything than what I'm doing, I *love* it here! Why wouldn't I like it?"

But Ray knew something that I didn't know. He knew that my past wasn't who I was. He knew that my report cards weren't who I was. He knew that the results that I was getting in my paycheck weren't who I really was.

He asked, "What do you really want?"

I said, "I want some money."

Money really was all I wanted then. You see, I was earning $4,000 a year, but I owed $6,000. If I took everything I earned for eighteen months to pay off my debt, with nothing left to live on, I would have just broken even.

Ray pulled a wad of cash out of his pocket and said, "This stuff can't talk but it can hear, and if you call it, it will come. How much do you want?"

"$25,000."

However, I absolutely did not believe I could earn $25,000. I mean, we would have had to sell one of the aerial ladders to come up with that kind of money. No one I knew had $25,000 . . . that would have been like swimming to Hawaii. It wasn't possible. I had been raised to believe it was not possible. I had it right in my bones not to believe that. Nobody in our family had ever done anything like that. As far back as you could go, nobody had ever even gone to school in our family. I had no idea how that ridiculous, impossible amount of money came into my head and out of my mouth.

Ray didn't bat an eyelash, though. He simply said to me, "If you do exactly as I tell you, I'll show you exactly how to get what you want."

I didn't believe it. But I believed *he* believed it—and that touched something inside of me.

So I decided I would do what he said, starting with reading the book he handed me, a book I'd never heard of, called *Think and Grow Rich* by Napoleon Hill.

Ray said to me, "I want you to study every day." That was a difficult thing for me to do, but I did it. I decided I would do exactly what he told me until I found out that he was lying or that he didn't know what he was talking about.

And like I said, my whole world began to change. It began to change like night and day. I started to look around. I would see my fellow firemen coming in to the firehouse and sitting down in front of the television set. They were maybe in their forties and they were talking about the union and getting an early retirement. And then I'd hear that Harry, who had just retired last year, had died this morning. Poor bugger. His heart just stopped beating.

And I thought, *I can't stay here. I've got to get out of here.* So I continued to do what Ray told me. And I've never stopped.

Today, if I coach somebody, it's the same deal. You must do exactly what I suggest until you find out I'm lying or I don't know what I'm talking about.

That's the deal for you, too. I know you'll think I'm a little crazy, and probably in the mind of the masses, I am.

But if you do exactly what I tell you, you'll get the results that you want. Just like I did.

If you're managing people, don't let their behavior screw up your head. Don't let what they're getting cause you to think that's what they're capable of. Get them to believe what *you* believe. How do you get them to do that? Just get them to do some simple things. But get them to commit. Get them to do it every day. *Every* day. There's no trick to this. This has nothing to do with whether you're smart or not.

# YOU NEED ONLY ONE QUALITY

*The Life-Changing Power of Discipline*

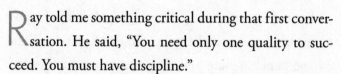

Ray told me something critical during that first conversation. He said, "You need only one quality to succeed. You must have discipline."

Well, I didn't want to have discipline. I didn't know what the word meant. I had been in the Canadian Navy, and it was something like when I had been in school. I wouldn't do what I was told, only in the navy if you didn't do what you were told, you were in deep trouble, I mean you paid for it! I was locked up on my twenty-first birthday, and they had me going through assault courses all day.

Oh, it was sadistic what they did to us. But I knew what the rules were. And I said, "Screw you. I'm not following your rules!" *Oh, aren't you?!* You know, I think they should take every young guy and stick him in the army or the Marines or something, for six months or a year, so he grows up fast. They toughen you up mentally!

Well, they toughened me up mentally, but they left me with the impression that discipline equaled punishment. If I didn't do what I was told, they would have me out on the parade square squatting with a rifle over my head. It was only a nine-pound rifle, but if you hold a nine-pound rifle over your head for even a few minutes, you think it weighs nine hundred pounds! And it's, "Get it up there!!"

"Yes sir, yes sir!"

I've only told this story once or twice but it just came to my mind, so I guess I'm supposed to tell you. I was out on the parade square and there was a petty officer in charge, and he was, in my opinion, mean. He had me hopping around on the parade square, and I had just finished fourteen days of this. I got out and they gave me another fourteen days, and I thought, *I can't handle this!* So I just fell over.

He said, "Get up!"

I said, "I can't, sir."

"What's the matter?"

I said, "I've got a pain in my side."

"Well then, go to sick bay," he said.

I told him I couldn't walk. Well, they got me to sick bay. And I was afraid to say I was lying, because then I'd really be in trouble! So they bring in this midshipman, and he was like an intern, only we were in the service. He pressed on my side and said, "Does it hurt?"

I said, "Yes sir."

The next morning, the surgeon took me in to have my appendix taken out! I was too afraid to tell them nothing was wrong! So they took my appendix out, I finished my punishment in the hospital and I got two weeks' sick leave. I thought, *I wish I had another appendix!*

Hey listen, when you don't play by the rules you get yourself into some funny spots. The point is, I had the idea that discipline was punishment. I thought *that* was discipline—get them out there in the parade square and beat the heck out of them.

The truth is, discipline is the ability to give yourself a command and then follow it. You will never develop anything of any consequence if you are not disciplined. If you are disciplined, you can have most anything you want. This is so basic, it's so simple and it's so misunderstood. Most people go through their entire life and never enjoy what they could enjoy because they lack discipline. But Ray was right—when you have discipline, you can have anything you seriously want.

I am a very disciplined person. I don't care if anybody else is working. I don't care what anyone else is doing. I know what I've got to do, and I get it done, and I don't need anybody to motivate me. I don't need anybody to praise me. I just need discipline. That's all. You don't need to throw me any bouquets. Just let me put my imagination to work, and I say, "I'm going to do this!" And I go and do it.

If you want to make any significant change in your life, you absolutely must command yourself to do what you know has to be done and then follow through. If you can do that, you'll get stronger and stronger. And then you'll be able to do what you want, instead of just what you think you can do.

# IF YOU CAN'T CLEAN ALL OF THEM, DON'T CLEAN ANY OF THEM

## *Shattering the Myth of Hard Work*

In the second chapter of my book *You Were Born Rich*, I tell people how to get out of debt. You set up an automatic debt repayment program, where a portion of your income automatically goes into an account. It's all looked after; it's all automatic; it's like an auto responder. It's an automatic way to pay debt so that you never have to think about debt. Then you start building the concept of prosperity in your mind.

You see, whatever you think about all the time, you will attract into your life. Not what you want—what you are emotionally involved with. Which is why if you have a goal of getting out of debt, you will probably stay in debt forever.

As I said earlier, I wasn't serious when I first blurted out my goal of making $25,000—at least not consciously so. But Ray took me seriously, and he had me write that goal down on a card.

Once I did that, something very interesting began to happen.

Before this, I was always thinking about debt. Creditors were forever phoning me and I'd say, "Get out of here! I don't have any money!" I would get angry at them even though it was their money! They shouldn't have lent it to me. But they did, you see, and surprise, they wanted it back. So, at any rate, I was spending all my time thinking about debt.

But once I wrote that goal down, I started thinking about earning money. That $25,000.

I had heard somebody say, "There's good money in cleaning floors." I thought, *I'm not proud. I'll clean floors.* That same person had also said, "Don't work for someone else; work for yourself." Made sense to me, but to do that I had to get a floor machine and other equipment.

I found a used machine for $980, and some buckets and mops to go with it, which meant I had to get $980. No one would lend me money—I wouldn't lend me money either, because I knew I wasn't going to pay it back! It's not that I didn't want to pay it back, it's that I never had enough money to pay it back. But I read in a book, if one person won't lend it, go to another person, and another person, and pretty soon you'll get good at your presentation and somebody will lend you the money.

That's how I ended up in a trust company and got in to see the manager, Al Keiper. There I am in Mr. Keiper's office, telling him what I want, and I'm enthusiastic, and I had built this business in my imagination and I was going to clean floors all over the world. I think he thought I was a little crazy, but I was also pretty enthusiastic about what I was going to do.

He said, "I'm going to lend you the money." I was shocked. But at any rate, I got the thousand dollars and away I went.

I had my cleaning business I was working at, along with my duties as a fireman. I thought the way to make more money was to work harder, get another office, then another. So here I am, cleaning offices, putting out fires, cleaning offices, putting out fires, cleaning offices. When I went into the firehouse I prayed no one would start a fire, I was so tired and wanted to sleep.

One day I passed out on the street. I was exhausted. I regained consciousness on the sidewalk, looked up, and there was a great big police officer looking down at me. He might not have been a very big man, but he looked like a giant to me when I was looking up at him, and it was a scary environment because there was a crowd of people around me and there were lights flashing and I could hear a siren. I had passed out, and I guess somebody thought I was dead. I was only about twenty-seven years old. It's not normal for a twenty-seven-year-old young man to pass out on the street.

They were going to take me to the hospital. I finally regained consciousness and realized where I was, and I thought, *I've got to get out of here.* So I talked them into not taking me to the hospital and I got away by myself, sat down somewhere and started to think. And suddenly, a quiet voice inside of me said, "If you can't clean all of them, don't clean any of them."

So I got all dressed up, and I got other people cleaning offices. And in less than five years, I was cleaning offices in Toronto, Montreal, Boston, Cleveland, Atlanta and London, England. If you had asked me what I was doing, I'd have said cleaning offices. But what else was I doing? I was reading *Think and Grow Rich* every day—in a disciplined manner. There were a lot of people cleaning offices, but they weren't doing what I was doing. There were a lot of people reading *Think and Grow Rich* but they weren't doing what I was doing. And all of a sudden, I wanted to know why I was enjoying all this success.

# THE PROBLEM IS WHERE YOU ARE

## *Moving Beyond Goal Setting*

One of the first lessons Ray Stanford taught me was that you have to look at where you are first and then where you're going, and then you have to get moving. That is so simple and so obvious. Yet if that's all there is to it—and there really *is* nothing else to it—then why are people so stuck?

The obvious thing is that they don't know where they are going. In other words, they don't have a goal.

I used to think that was the problem, but I don't

anymore. I believe that most people have a goal. They may not be very articulate when it comes to describing the goal, they may not have written it down so that anybody could understand it, but I think they've got some point they'd like to move toward.

So what does that leave? It leaves where you are. I've become aware that the problem is right here—where you are right now.

Where are you? Well, most people say, "I know where I am, I am here at the Sheraton Hotel at your seminar." Uh-huh. That's where you are physically. But where are you mentally? Why would someone who knows all this great information continue to have a conflict, continue to be nonproductive, continue to be stuck?

The answer is because there are two parts to our personality. There's a part that views the world and everything in it. That is our intellectual mind. It's the side where we have the ability to choose, think and imagine. And then there is the other part of our personality—the subconscious or emotional mind. We'll get to that in a bit.

I'd like for you to raise your hand if you believe you can earn a lot more money than you are right now. Well then, why the heck aren't you? You say, "I believe I can!"

And on one level you do believe it. On a conscious level, you say, "Yes, *yes*! I not only believe it, *I know it*!"

But that isn't the part of you that controls your behavior, and it's your behavior that controls the amount of money you earn.

The part of your personality that controls your behavior is not the part that I'm talking to right now. The part that I'm talking to now is your intellectual mind. You're sitting there thinking, *Well, I know that!* But what your intellectual mind probably doesn't know is that on a subconscious level, you do not believe that you can earn a lot more money.

The word "praxis" is the integration of belief with behavior. Our job is to help you take the ideas that you believe on a conscious level, and move them to your subjective mind. Move the old conditioned ideas out and move the new idea in. When that happens, everything changes.

I did that. I earned a whole lot of money, and I had no idea what I was doing.

See, paradigms are the problem. What is a paradigm? A paradigm is a multitude of habits—it's the programming in the subjective mind. We'll get into paradigms in a little bit.

❖

Ray Stanford sat me down and he put an "R" on a sheet of paper. He said, "Bob, let that 'R' represent the results that you are getting in your life. Are you happy with your results?"

Then he put two "H"'s and a "W" on the paper and said, "Let these two 'H''s and the 'W' represent happiness, health and wealth. Do you think I'm a happy guy?"

I said, "Yes, you seem pretty happy to me."

He said, "Have you ever seen me when I was sick?" I had to admit that I hadn't.

He said, "Have you *ever* seen me when I was broke?" This guy always had a roll of money on him. I never saw him when he was broke.

Then he said, "Bob, you've got to be one of the most miserable people I have ever met." And I was. I was an unhappy human being. I was unhappy almost all the time.

Oh, I had fun every now and then—but fun and happiness are two different things. Fun is very short-lived and it's very shallow. I think everybody has fun now and then. But happiness is something that runs very deep and it's long lasting. I wasn't a very happy person; I just didn't know it.

He said, "You are just flat-out miserable. You are. You're always sick. You don't have a terminal illness or anything, but you've always got a headache or a cold or something. And you're always broke."

Remember, I was earning $4,000 a year at the time, but I owed $6,000.

This is when he said, "Do exactly what I tell you to do."

I don't know why he picked me. Honest to God, I cannot tell you why. I'm pretty sure we have guides that are with us, and they help us along the road. I believe that I was guided and it wasn't an accident that this man was in my life.

In one year, I went from earning $4,000 and owing $6,000 to earning $175,000. I had absolutely no idea what the heck I was doing. Then I took it to over a million dollars. This was back in the 1960s, when a million dollars was a lot of money. It's a lot of money today, but relatively speaking, it's not that much. If you asked me what I was doing, I didn't know. I really did not know. However, as I have already mentioned, I had to know why I had changed.

You see, I came from such a messed-up background. I had never accomplished anything of any consequence. I have a brother and sister; they both did well in school.

They never got in trouble. My sister's a year older than me, my brother's a year younger. And things were always cool with them. With me, my mother used to cry, "Why are you doing this to me?" I wasn't doing anything to her, I was doing it to me! On top of the problems I was creating for myself, I was permitting her remarks to create guilt in my mind.

Then I went into the navy, as I said, and what an experience that was. I had no business experience. I had very little formal education—after eighth grade, I went to Danforth Technical School for just a couple of months. One day the vice principal called me into his office and informed me that my formal education had just come to an abrupt halt. I was so happy! It was all over. I didn't have to go back there anymore! To say I didn't like school was an understatement. No one had ever caused me to like school.

Let's think about this. When you leave school and go to work, what are you doing? You're selling your time, your energy, your loyalty, your knowledge for an amount of money. What the heck did I have to sell? I didn't even have a good attitude.

So I got a job, first of all, delivering groceries for a butcher shop. I had to deliver them on a wagon because I didn't have a bicycle. I soon burned out with that, and then I got a job in the downtown area of Toronto from five at night until two in the morning working at a printing shop for $12 a week. But looking back today, I realize that they were actually being kind because I wasn't even worth the $12.

After the navy I worked in bars. In fact, I worked in two bars where I only lasted an hour before they fired me. Now that's a bit of a record . . . to hold a job for only an hour. And I did it twice!

I remember I was driving by one of the places and I said to my wife, "Linda, see that place there—that was one of the places where I lasted just an hour." I was drinking more than I was selling! It just wasn't profitable to have me there.

So here I am with all these offices, all these people, earning all this money and thinking of my background, trying to figure out how I was doing it. If the contrast hadn't been as great as it was, I probably would have just continued on, opened more cleaning offices, and continued doing what I was doing. But it was so enormous that it started to puzzle me. I had to know what happened. Why did I change?

I was determined to find the answer. It took me nine years to figure it out. I had shifted my paradigm, that's what I had done. I shifted my paradigm in two ways. One way was my personal involvement in something that had an emotional impact on me, and the other was through the constant, spaced repetition of an idea.

# MONEY IS A MAGNIFIER

*How to Do What You Want to Do*

I have a handheld record player that I used to drive around with, playing the same two records over and over and over again—Earl Nightingale's recordings of *The Strangest Secret* and *Think and Grow Rich.* I listened to those records so many times that the messages were seared into my brain. They became an inseparable part of me. They changed me at the cellular level. I literally became those messages.

❖

I've met some of the most brilliant people in the world. I have studied with some absolute geniuses. And because I was so interested in what they were teaching, they were interested in teaching me. I know things that a lot of people never learn. I know why we do what we do, and why we *don't* do what we *want* to do. As simple and obvious as that sounds, very few people know why they don't do what they already know how to do, why their life is stuck.

❖

The first large company I worked with as a consultant was the Prudential of America. It was the largest insurance company in the history of the world—the largest! They spent millions of dollars on training. Yet they did not know why their stars were stars.

I knew why.

I ended up in Mel Haycraft's office, vice president of the Chicago office in the Prudential Center, the number one territory out of ten territories of that company. He said, "What have you got?"

I said, "I've got some ideas that I think will change your whole world."

"Really."

"Yes."

In response, he took a handful of brochures and threw them across the table. He had nothing on his desk but these brochures. And he said, "They all say the same thing."

"But I'm different."

"How are you different?"

I said, "I get results."

"Oh really? All these people said that too."

"Yeah, well, I'm different."

"What makes you different?"

"I make me different," I said. "Listen, we could stay here playing games forever. Your responsibility is to increase the sales. There's someone above you who is watching you and if you don't improve sales they are going to let you go. You know that. I am the guy who's going to help you do what you want to do. Give me a hundred of your best people—don't give me your worst, anyone can do something with your worst—give me your best people and I'll show you what I can do and I won't charge you a dime."

He looked at me and said, "I like that."

I said, "I thought you would."

He accepted my offer. We took 100 of his best people; we had them selling more than they had ever sold in the same period. Everybody in the company wanted to know what the heck Mel Haycraft was doing. After I did the 100-person test, I had 450 of Prudential's salespeople at the Hillside Holiday Inn in Chicago. I stood up in front of them and I told them, "I can show every one of you how to go out and write $5 million in business this year."

When I said that, I lost the whole audience. Their bodies stayed, but their minds left.

At the first break, a man came up to me and said, "Proctor, have you ever sold insurance?"

"No, I never have. Why?"

"You don't know what you're talking about."

"Oh, I know what I'm talking about. I just said I've never sold insurance."

He said, "Do you know this company is going to be one hundred years old next year?"

"That's right."

"Do you know we've got twenty thousand sales agents?"

"Yes."

"Do you know we've never had one write $5 million?"

"Then you can be the first."

He looked at me with sort of a smirk on his face. "You said we could do it this year. It's August, the year's over half gone."

I said, "Then it isn't going to take you as long to do it, is it?

"Here's the deal," I said. "You already know how to write the $5 million. Your problem isn't how to write it. Your problem is—why aren't you doing what you already know how to do? If you go back in there and open your ears and listen to me, I'm going to show you how to write $5 million. I don't have to sell insurance to know how to do that. You know how to sell the insurance. You don't know why you're not doing what you want to do."

His name was Don Slovan. The second week in December he had $5,200,000 worth of business on the books. He closed the year with a little over $6 million. This is all in Prudential's records. I've got it in magazines I could show you.

He wasn't the only one to sell $5 million in insurance. There was a whole string of people who followed him. They sent psychologists out from New Jersey to try and figure out what this guy Proctor was doing! One psychologist went back and said, "Record what he's doing, we'll go out and get an actor to teach what he's doing!" I thought,

*That poor guy, he doesn't even know what I'm doing.* He thought it was what I was saying. It wasn't what I was saying at all. It was the energy that I was putting out.

I figured out what I had done to change my life. I didn't have to study anyone's personality to show them how to change. I just had to study mine. I don't have to study you. I just have to study me. We are all the same. Some are male, some are female, but outside of the reproductive system, we're all the same. You might think of age, race and cultural differences. The only difference there is in appearance and the truth is rarely in the appearance of things. Throw us all into a hot fire and we are all reduced to the same level. Use your higher faculties. Look within.

We are spiritual beings, living in a physical body. There is only one mind. Just one. We all have the same mental faculties. We all have different programming. We all have different genetic conditioning. We were all raised in different environments. But we all have the same faculties.

We are conditioned to live through our senses. We can hear, see, smell, taste and touch. We let the outside world control our mind. We look at our report card and let it control what we are like. The report card turns into our sales sheet or our job evaluation.

We have been gifted with the higher mental faculties of intuition, perception, will, memory, reason and imagination. When we begin developing and effectively using these faculties, we can control our outside world and stop letting it control us.

Einstein was so right when he said, "The intuitive mind is a sacred gift and the rational mind is a faithful servant. We have created a society that honors the servant and has forgotten the gift."

What we have to do is gain an understanding of how our programming took place, and how we can change it so that it stops controlling us and we start to control ourselves. When you do that, that's when you take control of your life. That's when you can set any goal and get there.

There is only one problem in the world, and that is ignorance. The only problem in your company is ignorance. The only thing holding people back is ignorance. People just don't know. And they don't know they don't know, in most cases.

As we go through these classes together, you're going to find that your life starts to shift. All you are going to do is open up—become more aware.

Look at what Napoleon Hill said. This is so good.

When money comes in quantities known as "big money," it flows to the one who accumulates it, as easily as water flows downhill. There exists a great unseen stream of *power*, which may be compared with a river, except that one side flows in one direction, carrying all who get into that side of the stream onward and upward to *wealth*—and the other side flows in the opposite direction, carrying all who are unfortunate enough to get into it (and not able to extricate themselves from it) downward to misery and *poverty*.

Every person who has accumulated a great fortune has recognized the existence of this stream of life. It consists of one's *thinking process*. The positive emotions of thought form the side of the stream that carries one to fortune. The negative emotions form the side that carries one down to poverty.

This carries a thought of stupendous importance to

the person who is following this with the object of accumulating a fortune.

If you are in the side of the stream of power that leads to poverty, this may serve as an oar by which you may propel yourself over into the other side of the stream. It can serve you *only* through application and use. Merely reading, and passing judgment on it one way or another, will in no way benefit you.

Poverty and riches often change places. Poverty may, and generally does, voluntarily take the place of riches. When riches take the place of poverty, the change is usually brought about through well-conceived and carefully executed *plans*. Poverty needs no plan. It needs no one to aid it, because it is bold and ruthless. Riches are shy and timid. They have to be "attracted."

We want to focus on big money. We want to get ourselves in the flow of big money. We want to start talking about big money. I talk a lot about money, trying to provoke people to think about it in the right sense. But know this: Money is a magnifier. That's all it is. Earning a lot of money doesn't make you a better person; it makes you more of what you already are. If you're not a nice person, you'll become unbearable. If you are a nice person, you'll become a nicer person. Money enables you to do more of what you love to do. That's really what it's for. Money does only two things: one, it is used to make you more comfortable, and the more comfortable you are, the more effective you become; and two, it enables you to extend the good you do far beyond your physical presence.

Where does the money come from? From the infinite. Where does everything come from? Think about it. Money is just paper. That's all it is, paper with ink on it. It's as useless as old newspaper until you go to use it. Physical paper isn't money. It *represents* money. Money is an idea. All the money in the universe is available to you. But you've got to attract it. It has to be earned. The only people who "make" money are in jail, in the Mint or on their way to jail. Everybody else earns it. It's that simple. There's nothing complicated about this. It's all rather simple if we stop and learn it.

Think of it this way: If you start your day off right, thinking optimistically, odds are pretty good that it will stay right. On the flip side, if you start your day off wrong, thinking negatively, odds are good it will stay wrong. You can be pretty certain that you won't be very far into your day and somebody's going to try and ruin it. They're going to give you bad news. Maybe you look at a newspaper and see something bad. Turn your television on, bad news. Someone will try and disturb you. They're not consciously and deliberately trying to do it. That's their way of life. That's how they live. If you listen to them, you are going to be off track. You must get on the right track.

That's the way it is with money.

I want you to visualize it. Build that picture of the river in your mind. One side is carrying you toward what you want. The other side is carrying you away from what you want. One side is taking you to wealth, the other side is taking you to poverty.

# YOU ARE THE SUM TOTAL OF YOUR THOUGHTS

## *Energy, Awareness and the Real Key to Change*

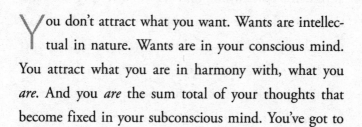

You don't attract what you want. Wants are intellectual in nature. Wants are in your conscious mind. You attract what you are in harmony with, what you *are*. And you *are* the sum total of your thoughts that become fixed in your subconscious mind. You've got to get the want and plant what you want in your heart of hearts. You've got to plant it deep in the universal subconscious mind. That will then dictate the vibration you are in, and you can only attract energy to you that's in harmonious vibration with you. Levels of vibration are called frequencies. Our mind and body function on frequencies. Just like your radio, it can only receive from the frequency it is operating on. If you are disturbed, if you are letting things bother you, if you are letting financials bother you, I can guarantee you, as sure as it's going to get dark outside tonight, you're going to attract more problems. You can only attract what you are in harmony with.

Now, you ask, how do you change that?

You change it through awareness. It's like when you were a little kid in school and the teacher's trying to teach you a new mathematical equation when you've just learned how to multiply and then they throw fractions at you. You not only multiply the number, they put a line under the number and a number under the line. And then they put these stacked numbers next to each other and tell you to multiply them. Of course you don't know what you're doing. The teacher shows you on the board, but you didn't get it so the teacher comes over to you and she does an equation. You still don't get it because you are so nervous. She asks if you are paying attention. Then, she asks you to do it.

You say, "I don't know how."

The teacher says, "I just showed you."

You repeat, "I don't know how."

The teacher says, "Well, pay attention. Watch what I'm showing you."

You see, you weren't listening. You hear with your ears but you listen with your emotions. Frequently, someone will be talking to you and you will hear them, but if they ask you what they said you couldn't repeat it. You must let yourself become emotionally involved with what they are saying. So now you listen as the teacher goes through it again, and finally you say, "Now I see!" And away you go. Awareness kicks in . . . you understand.

You must develop the awareness. And awareness must have a foundation. Understanding is your foundation. That is precisely why King Solomon centuries ago said, "With all thy getting get understanding."

Now let's think—let's really think. The results you're getting are an expression of your level of awareness. If you let this fall into place in your mind, I think you're going to find that your awareness is blocked by paradigms. It's old conditioning that blocks the awareness. You've got to change the conditioning.

Now imagine if your awareness expanded a little bit—just imagine if that happened. My goodness, if that's all you did, you could multiply your results! It is important that you understand this to expand your level of conscious awareness—and that's all we're doing here is expanding your level of awareness in different areas.

You eliminate the darkness when you turn on the light. Let there be light—let there be a higher level of conscious awareness.

Listen, a person doesn't earn $100,000 a year because they want to earn $100,000 a year. They earn $100,000 a year because they are not aware of how to earn $100,000 a month! When they become aware of how to earn $100,000 a month, they're not going to go back and settle for $100,000 a year.

Let there be light. Let there be a higher degree of consciousness. We want to expand our level of awareness. It's like Maya Angelou said: "Do the best you can until you know better. Then when you know better, do better."

Why would people struggle? People don't want to

struggle. They're struggling because they're not aware of how to eliminate the struggle.

How do you expand your level of awareness? Now that's a good question. And it's a question that everybody should get an answer to. You do it through effective education combined with professional coaching over a reasonable period of time. You'll alter the conditioning and expand your level of awareness.

See, expanding your awareness is simply putting a bigger idea in the place of the smaller idea. Each time you do that you become more aware of how it's done.

We say it's a sad thing when a child is afraid of the dark. But I'll tell you something that's a lot sadder than that: an adult who's afraid of the light. Some people are afraid of waking up. They are so comfortable where they are—do you know there are women right around here, probably within walking distance of where you are right now, who are being bounced off the wall by some brute or some drunken beast every night? And they're afraid to leave!! Why are they afraid to leave? Because they're more afraid of being on their own than they are of being with this guy. Sometimes when they do leave they go right back into the same thing again. This is not uncommon. What's doing it? It's their consciousness that's doing it. You've got to shift the consciousness. If you don't, you can't make a permanent change. You can't attract what you really want.

*Everything we are seeking is seeking us.*

When I first read that, I know I didn't understand it. Everything we are seeking is seeking us. Awareness is the name of the game. So we're going to become aware of certain things about ourselves.

[Bob chose a person at random and described her personality in detail.]

**BOB:** Tina, how long have you studied the human personality? How many years?

**TINA:** Twenty-six years.

**BOB:** How often do you run into somebody who can just walk by and tell you what you're like, the way I did earlier? It's unusual, isn't it?

TINA: It is rare.

BOB: This is the first time you've ever run into anybody like that. Yet I was very accurate. I could go further just to validate the accurateness, but I am very accurate in reading your personality, aren't I?

TINA: You're very accurate.

BOB: How would I know how to do that? Well listen, what you see sitting here is not Tina. This is Tina's body. This is a molecular structure. It's a mass of molecules in a very high speed of vibration. Her mind is movement. This is not her mind, this is the expression of her mind. The mind is movement. Body is the manifestation of that movement. Now, the vibration she's in—I pick it up. I can read that vibration. If I can read it, you can read it. If I had my eyes closed, I'd know what she's like, all right? The energy coming from the body is so potent and powerful, it will penetrate a camera, penetrate a film, and you can actually photograph the energy. As Tina changes the images in her mind, the density in the color of the energy will change.

The year I was born—a *long* time ago—Semyon Kirlian, a Russian photographer, perfected a form of photography where you can photograph a mass and you can photograph the energy coming from it. So as Tina changes the images in her mind, the density and the color of the images will change.

Now as I come in contact with her energy, I can cause her energy to change. In fact, I will cause her energy to change—and she would cause mine to change. Neither one of us knows anything about this, we're just, let's say, a couple of office workers, but our energy is causing the other person's energy to change.

Take any office in any company where people are sitting at their desks. I could walk into such an office and I could say, "Move that woman back there," "Move that man over here," "Take this lady and put her over here"— I could rearrange the office and productivity would go up in the office. I'd get energy flowing freely. It's called "circulation."

When the blood in the body stops circulating you're done. It's all over. You'll move on to the next phase of your eternal journey. Circulation is the law of the universe. Well, when you get the energy in an office flowing freely, productivity is going to go up. We've got to be aware that our environment has a whole lot to do with our mental state.

-:⋄:-

Karl Menninger from the Menninger Foundation in To- peka, Kansas, said environment is more important than heredity. You have to be very careful about the people you spend time with. I am very, very careful with the people I spend a lot of time with. There are some people I just don't want to spend a lot of time around. I don't think I'm any better than them, I just don't want to be like them. I don't think I'm better than anybody, and I don't think anybody is better than me. But I'll tell you something—I don't want to live the life that some people are living and if you don't want to live the way they are living, get away from them. You would be wise not to spend a lot of time with somebody who is in a bad vibration all the time.

BOB: Now, Tina, you have been studying the mind for twenty-some years and yet you say it's very unusual how I can walk by a person and tell you all about them. Here's the point I want to get across—this abil- ity is not unique—it's just unusual relative to most people. If I can do something, you can do it. I don't have anything going for me that you haven't got going for you! You can learn how to do what you witness others doing if you really want to and you are prepared to pay the price.

When I walk into a boardroom in a corporate office, I know exactly what the people in the boardroom are like and exactly how to work with everyone at the table. I know the ones who are very left-brained and those who are very right-brained, and those who bounce between left- and right-brained. I pay attention to their energy, and I know just how to structure the conversation so that I make the sale. In my mind, it's not a matter of whether I'm *going* to make the sale, it's do I *want* to make the sale? And if I don't want to make the sale, I'm not going to make it. Why? Well, there are some people you just don't want to work with. I'm not going to work with somebody where I have to keep selling them every day. Why would you want to coach somebody where you have to keep selling them every day? If they don't do what I say, then we are both toast. So I am selective about who I work with. Most people want you to coach them their way and their way is not working.

As long as a client does what I say, I'll keep going. They'll earn multi-millions of dollars if that's what they really want and they remain a great student. But often they will learn only so much and then they don't want to learn any more from you, so they shut down.

Great students gather information very quickly. Great students always want more. They are eager to learn. They soak it up. Avi is a great student of mine. He is forever asking me questions—about this, about that. Little things. He's not embarrassed to ask any kind of question.

There are no dumb questions. If you've got a question, you should ask it. The objective is to develop awareness. It's all about awareness. That's all there is.

# YOU'VE ALREADY GOT IT

*Understanding Your Spiritual Perfection*

In his book *Working with the Law*, Raymond Holliwell wrote, "There is a marvelous inner world that exists within us, and the revelation of such a world enables us to do, to attain and to achieve anything we desire within the bounds or limits of Nature."

There's a world operating within you. A wonderful world. We want to try and understand that. Your spiritual DNA is perfect. It's absolutely perfect. It requires no modification, no improvement. There is absolute perfection within you. It is really important that we get this. *There is perfection within you.* It doesn't have to be modified. It doesn't have to be changed. It's there. All you have to do is let it come to the surface. When you stretch and go for something you really love that is beyond what you think you can do, you will find that you can perform a whole lot better than you used to think you could. You became aware that there is the ability within that you previously failed to recognize.

You see, we operate on the idea that you have to get "it," whatever "it" is . . . to become whatever you want to be. You don't have to "get" anything. You've *got* it. I didn't get anything to go from being broke and struggling to earning millions. I just became aware of what I already had.

Science and theology teach us that all the power that ever was is always present in all places at the same time. That it is within me! It's ever present—all the power—all the knowledge. Let's try to understand that. All the knowledge there ever was or ever will be is 100 percent evenly present in all places at the same time. That's a big idea. Nothing is created or destroyed. Everything is made from the same thing: spirit/energy. Ask yourself, "Where do ideas come from?" "Where did the idea for the smart phone come from?"

The simple truth is that a person activated their imagination and originated the idea from the power that is continually flowing to and through us. That person was aware that if they could see it in their mind, they could hold it in their hand.

This is not difficult. This is really pretty easy to understand. I taught this to kids.

I was showing a friend a picture hanging on my wall in my home. It's a set of five sports cards in a frame. Each card has a picture of one of the five living gold medal decathlon winners at that time and each of them was signed by the gold medal winner. A good friend of mine, Milt Campbell, was one of them. He was the one who gave me these cards. The others are Bob Mathias, Jim Thorpe, Rafer Johnson, and Bruce Jenner (now known as Caitlyn Jenner).

Milt was working with me at the time. We had a group of twelve kids. I worked with them for one hour a week on the phone. I was teaching them about their mind and about their life. They were on the stage in Kansas City in front of approximately ten thousand people after just twelve weeks—twelve one-hour lessons on the phone—and the adults were taking notes. It was absolutely mind-blowing what those kids learned about their mind in such a short time.

Adults—we think we know so much—so we reject all this as "woo-woo." These truths have always been here and understood by a few.

❖

Just understand that you're a spiritual being. There is a power flowing to and through you and you can do whatever you want with it. And as it flows in, you choose thoughts. As you internalize those thoughts you alter the vibratory rate of the body. On a conscious level, as we become aware of the vibration we are in, we refer to that conscious awareness as *feeling* . . . "feeling" is a word we have invented to describe conscious awareness of vibration.

Let's take a look at this another way—it's a matter of choice. Look at what Holliwell says about this: "All failures in life are due to taking sides with the finite around us. All success in life is due to taking sides with the law within."

If we can't see it, smell it, taste it or touch it, if we can't get involved with the physical, we say it's not there. You know, often you hear people say, "What you don't know won't hurt you." Well, what you don't know can kill you. Stop and think about this. There's air in this room. If we sealed it all up airtight and then started to pump air in, what would happen? We'd blow the room up. We would literally blow all the walls out of the place.

There is a power in what you cannot see. We've got to start to understand this. *All failures in life are due to us taking sides with the finite*—with what's going on outside. We see a limitation on the outside and so we think we can't have something different. We want more money, but we see the dwindling bank account. So we stop pursuing what we really want. You see, if we put our focus on the finite around us, such as the dwindling bank account, and believe it is the truth for us, that is what we will get more of.

However, we can shift our focus to the inside and the success we want and believe that is possible for us. It doesn't matter what you want to learn . . . the way to do it is already here. If you are stuck, it's only because you're not aware of what's already here. Keep thinking . . . imagine whatever it is. See it completed. The way will come either through ideas you think or through another person. By seeing it completed you have flipped your mind onto the frequency that contains the way and it will be attracted to you.

I often stand in a seminar, point at myself, and say, "This is me." But the truth is *this* isn't me at all. This is my body. If you ask, "Who are you?" I say, "I'm Bob." I'm not Bob. Bob is my name. You've never heard anyone say, "Am hand. Am head. Am foot." You say, "My hand, my head, my foot. My name. My body." This isn't *me*. You will never see the real me with your physical eyes. I am all knowing. I am all powerful. Part of me is everywhere because I am a soul. I don't have a soul, I am a soul. I am spirit. I am God's highest form of creation.

Think about it. You can feel another person's presence even if they are on the other side of the world. If they are thinking of you and you are thinking of them and you are emotionally involved with their energy—you're in harmony with them, on the same frequency—then you will feel their presence. This is because there is no time or space in spirit. It's an illusion that there is. When it comes to the mind, there isn't any time or space. We've got to try and understand this.

We've got to understand that all the knowledge that ever was or ever will be is always here. The way to fly airplanes has always been here. The way to build microphones and computers has always been here. Why do people struggle? Why do they always resist this type of information? When Henry Ford built cars it was not uncommon to hear a person say, "I am not buying one of those dumb things." "You'd be much better off getting a good horse and a fine buggy!" "People will never buy those things!!" "You would have to build roads and have gas for the cars on every corner." "Cars will never catch on."

Today, we think cars are the best way to travel. But the truth is the *best* way to travel hasn't even been thought of yet. The best way to do what you're doing has never been thought of yet. Why don't you think of it? Why don't you think of a better way to communicate this information? The information is here. All you need to do is tap into it.

Recently, I went to Tel Aviv, from Tel Aviv to Cyprus, from Cyprus to Dubai, from Dubai to Melbourne, from Melbourne to Auckland, from Auckland to Los Angeles and from Los Angeles back to Toronto. This was all in about seven to eight days. Everywhere I went there were big crowds asking me, "Could I just spend an hour with you?" "Could I just spend fifteen minutes with you?" "Could I just ask you a question?" And I couldn't. I had to say "I can't" because I had to catch a plane; I had to go to the next city. But all the time I was thinking, *I should be able to spend time with those people. If I could just answer their questions, I could change their whole life. I probably know what they want to find out.* I thought, *There has got to be a way with the communication systems we've got today.*

So I'm flying from Los Angeles back to Toronto and I thought, *Streaming!* Well, I didn't know anything about streaming, so I called Joshua Carr, our IT guy, and said, "What do you know about streaming?"

He said, "Well, what do you want to know?"

I said, "Can I stream?"

He said, "Sure you can. I'll set it up."

About an hour or two later he phoned me back and said, "There's an icon on your computer, just click it." And just like that, I'm streaming. Within two hours of thinking of the idea, I had over three hundred people registered from sixty different countries who joined Bob Proctor's Streaming Club.

*There is no end to what you can do!!* But you've got to

step out and do it! I didn't know how to do that. I didn't have to know how to set that up. Somebody else knew how to do it. I got *them* to do it for me. What you've got to understand is that the way to do it is already here. All you need is some help.

*Get help!* Don't be afraid to ask for help. Humble yourself. Don't try to be the smartest person in town. You're not the smartest. There's always someone smarter. There are people who know how to do things that you don't know how to do. You can learn or get someone who knows how, as I did. But understand this too: we don't put ourselves down just because we don't know.

Andrew Carnegie put it perfectly when he said:

> *The accumulation of great fortunes calls for power, and power is acquired through highly organized and intelligently directed specialized knowledge, but that knowledge does not, necessarily, have to be in the possession of the [person] who accumulates the fortune.*

Andrew Carnegie stated that he personally knew nothing about the steel business, and he did not necessarily care to know anything about it. He found the specialized knowledge that he required for the manufacturing and marketing of steel through his mastermind group. It's worth mentioning that in 1908 Andrew Carnegie was the wealthiest man in the world, presumably the first billionaire.

All the power in the universe is 100 percent evenly present in all places at the same time. You've got it! You've got *all* the knowledge. *Every* question has an answer. Webster called a rhetorical question a question without an answer. That's not a question. That's a statement. Every question has an answer! The answer is on the flip side of the coin! There is the law of polarity. That law states that everything has an opposite. Question–answer; up–down; hot–cold. You can't have one without the other. Start asking yourself the right questions. The answers will be there.

You have got to ask yourself: "Are you truly what you pretend to be?"

We hear people say, "Ah, it's just me." Just me—*come on!* Or they say, "I'd really like to do it, but I don't know how I'll do it."

Have you any idea where we would be if people always said, "I can't do it because I don't know how?" You don't *have* to know how! You just have to know that you can.

If you set a goal and you know how to achieve it, you're not growing. You're going sideways! When you set a goal you should be setting a goal for something you have *absolutely* no idea how to do. The only prerequisite is: Do you want it? Do you *really* want it?

I tell a story in my book *You Were Born Rich*—this was back in the eighties—about a couple I knew. Pat and John were very disturbed; they weren't getting along; they were having a hard time. I said, "You know what your problem is? You don't have a goal! You need a goal. What's something you really want?"

She was sort of getting tuned in to our conversation, and he was getting angry with my questions.

Finally they said, "Well, we'd like to buy our own home."

I said, "Then go out and buy one."

He said, "But we don't have any money."

I said, "You don't need any money, what do you need money for?"

He said, "What do you mean, we don't need any money?"

I said, "Well, you haven't decided to buy the house so what do you need the money for?

"Let's really play with your mind. What do you really want?" They were living in a basement with her daughter at the time. His son wouldn't speak to him; he lived with his mother. They said they wanted to be together in their own house for Christmas and have his son and her daughter there with them.

I said, "OK then, that's the goal. That shouldn't be too hard to pull off. Just ask for it."

"Just ask for it?"

"Yeah, just ask for it!"

I called a real estate agent I knew, Natalie Kopman at Harvey Kalles Real Estate, whose office was nearby, and I said, "Come on over here. I've got a live one for you. They want to buy a house and they haven't got any money."

Natalie came over and she'd been to my seminar, so she knew exactly what to do. She said to them, "Describe the house for me." They described the house, and she went and found it. It was 7 Bards Walkway. She told them what they needed to get it. This was in October.

They both sold life insurance for the same company, and I said, "Go on and ask your manager how you can earn that much money in a hurry to put down." And they did it. They got into 7 Bards Walkway. They got in around the 10th or 12th of December, and I went to see them around the 16th.

They were in the house, but they had a little tiny table and just two chairs. I said, "How are you going to have Christmas dinner with this?"

They said, "John's son is still not talking to us."

I said, "Well, it's not Christmas yet!" As it so happened, my wife, Linda, and I had recently moved, and we had a spare dining room set we were looking to get rid of. I had this white Cadillac convertible and here I was driving down the parkway with the top down in the middle of winter, with the dining room set in the convertible. I had chairs wrapped around me, tables . . . but I got them there. And on Christmas day, his son showed up, her daughter was there, and they all had Christmas dinner together in their house.

There is something inside of you that wants to become *one* with that which *is*, with God. That desire is going to cause you to grow. When you let that something inside of you express itself through you, you become very creative.

You will want to start expressing your uniqueness as a human being. I know that I have answers to everything I want to know inside of me. I just have to relax my mind. I just have to open myself to the good I desire.

Sandy Gallagher, my business partner, and I sat down and we set a goal of earning $100 million a year with our company. Some people say, "Why don't you retire?" That's like saying, "Well, why don't you go and bury yourself!" Retirement is a bad idea—it's a pullback from life! It's a bad idea because I want to do a whole bunch of things. I want to build a whole bunch of schools in Africa. There are all kinds of things I want to do and it costs a whole lot of money. If you have more money than you need, then you're not doing what you should be doing! I've always got something more to do than what I've already done or accomplished.

I'm not really that interested in money outside of earning more, because of what I want to do with it. Money is just the vehicle. It's like the car that will get me home, the plane that will get me to where I want to go. Money is an instrument. It's an instrument that's used to express your uniqueness as a human being.

You are the offspring of a deathless soul. If you get

these things straight in your mind and understand that, then you're going to understand who the real you is. Get that straight. Get it straight in your mind.

You see, all you've done is just listen to what I'm saying and it's caused you to look at yourself a little more objectively, a little more like a stranger would.

We're the only creature on this planet that can have a look outside our self like a stranger might. We can observe our own behavior. We can listen to what we say. We can pay attention to what we're doing and where we're going. There isn't anybody alive who knows what you are capable of doing.

I've got a quote here from a friend of mine, Steve Bow. He said, "God's gift to us is more talent and ability than we'll ever hope to use in our lifetime. Our gift to God is to develop as much of that talent and ability as we can in this lifetime."

Before we finish here, you're going to have an opportunity to have everybody in this room help you get what you want. Now, you might not know what you want. Or you might have come in here thinking you knew what you wanted and it might have changed. It might have changed dramatically.

When you came here last time, Jennifer, you didn't know what you wanted, did you? No, you didn't. When was the last time you were here? The end of October—and this is just the middle of January. In the middle of October when you were leaving here, you were sort of down a little because everybody else pretty much knew what they wanted and you didn't know what you wanted. Then you got home and *wham!*, something happened. What happened? You stopped thinking, *What can I do?* and started thinking, *What am I really good at and love doing?* What are you good at?

**JENNIFER:** I'm a good mom, I love being a mom.

**BOB:** Then what?

**JENNIFER:** I am good because I take what you teach and apply it.

**BOB:** So you're managing motherhood? And what did you do?

**JENNIFER:** I decided I wanted to write a book in one week and make it a best seller by the next Matrixx seminar. I wrote you because I didn't want you to shoot it down. You said go for it. I contacted Peggy McColl.

**BOB:** And you wrote it in a week?

**JENNIFER:** Yes.

**BOB:** And is it good?

**JENNIFER:** Number one international best seller.

You see, she stopped thinking about what she couldn't do and started thinking about what she loved doing. Thanks, Jennifer. Give her another hand.

If you haven't decided what you want to do, forget about what you want to do. Ask yourself, "What do I *love* to do?"

I love doing this, I love it, I absolutely *love* it. I *love* watching people wake up! And when they do, you know it. They might not say anything, but you feel the energy— you *feel* the energy shift. You really do. You say, "Wow!" And I see that happening all the time in the room. That jazzes me. That really gets me going. This is a form of entertainment. That's what entertainers do. They put the energy out; they get the energy from the audience; they give the energy to the audience. They circulate it. That's what happens here in the room. And it keeps getting bigger and bigger and better and better.

What do you really love doing? What do you *really* love doing? We're going to get to the point where you're going to write your goal on a little card. You're going to realize it's not a big deal. Looking back, it becomes the best seller. It's sort of disgusting how simple it is, isn't it? I mean, you wonder, why make a big deal out of anything? It's a big deal because you don't know how to do it. If you're waiting until you figure out how to do it, you may never do anything. You just have to get going and help will come.

Jennifer didn't know anything about writing a best-selling book, so she asked me. I gave her Peggy McColl's number and she got hold of Peggy. Peggy's really good at books, writing them and making them best sellers.

How would you like to come up with an idea and have everyone here use all the connections and ideas they've got to help you? That would be kind of cool, wouldn't it? That's exactly what's going to happen. But they can't help you unless you decide what you want. You've got to have it written out. And if you give it to me to read, I'd have the same picture in my mind that you had in your mind as you wrote it. Is this a good idea? I think so.

# THE EXISTING MODEL IS OBSOLETE

*Reprogramming Your Mind for*
*Posttraumatic Growth*

Tina asked me a good question. I'll bring it out in front of everybody. She said, "There's posttraumatic stress and posttraumatic growth. How do you get involved with posttraumatic growth?"

Michael Beckwith gave me the answer to that. There's a three-step approach—in fact, I think he made a movie of it or wrote a book on it. There's a three-step approach to let go of the past and expect good in the future:

Number 1: *It is what it is—accept it.* It doesn't matter what has happened in your life. Some of you have had bad things happen in your past, really disturbing, they really messed your life up. *It is what it is, accept it.* Either you're going to control it, or it's going to control you. It is what it is, accept it.

I learned that from Michael on a Saturday. The following week, they had me in Cedars-Sinai Medical Center, cutting my chest open, taking my heart out, collapsing my lung and replacing the aortic valve. And do you want to know something? I got better, just like that, and I was back out on the road in ninety days going like a rocket because Michael had explained that to me on Saturday. He spoke on Saturday, I spoke on Sunday. I wrote down what he said. I thought, *This is brilliant.*

Number 2: *Harvest the good.* I love the word "harvest"—you can just see them bringing in the crops, you know? Harvest the good. There's good in everything and the more you look for it, the more you'll find. Harvest the good.

Number 3: *Forgive all the rest.* Forgive means to let go of it completely. Abandon. Just let it go. Quit dwelling on what's wrong. Forgive all the rest.

That's posttraumatic growth. There's the bad and the good.

You may be thinking, *Well, there's got to be more to it than that. I mean, I need to see a few behavioral scientists and psychiatrists and psychologists. I mean, we've got to go into a lot of therapy.*

See, you don't want to complicate it. If this were complicated, I would never have gotten it. I'm a simple guy. I'm really a simple guy. Just keep it simple. That's what you want to do. Reduce it to the ridiculous. It is what it is. Accept it. It's either going to control you, or you're going to control it. Number two—harvest the good. Number three—forgive all the rest.

I met Cynthia Kersey at the Airport Marina Hotel. I don't know if you know Cynthia Kersey, but she is a neat woman. She really is. She's raised millions of dollars to build schools all over the world. But at this particular moment I'm talking about, her husband had left her and she was pretty shaken up. She had just come back from her therapist to the hotel and I met her for the first time.

I said, "So what did your therapist have to say?"

Cynthia said, "Well, she said I was going to be really angry for nine months to a year."

I said, "What would you want to do that for?! Fire the therapist. Why would you want to be angry? Send him love." She looked at me like I'd fallen out of a tree.

She asked, "Send him love?"

I said, "Send him love. It's got nothing to do with him. While you are holding bad thoughts about him, he's probably out having a good time, and you're the one in the bad vibration!

"Start to understand how your mind functions. When you send him love it's got to pass through you. You take an energy that flows into your mind that has no form and you're giving it form. You turn it into something beautiful and you send it off to him. Whatever he does with it is up to him. But it's you that you're benefiting."

Do you know what forgiveness is? Forgiveness is for your benefit. You do something and I forgive you, that's for my benefit. I'm not doing it for you, I'm doing it for *me*! Forgive means to let go of completely. Abandon.

People keep repeating their sad stories over and over. They just keep living with the same sad stories. They keep repeating them. And you know what happens? If you keep repeating them, it's going to keep reoccurring, at least in your mind, if not in your physical world. Why do you want to live there? Did you like it? No. Well, why do you go there? Why don't you go where you want to go? You've got the ability to go wherever you want. You have the ability to choose.

You see, you're a spiritual being. The way you use your intellect dictates your emotional state. Whatever we get emotionally involved with determines the vibration that we're in. The body is a mass of molecules in a high speed of vibration.

Forgiveness is a phenomenal concept. Like I said, it means let go completely. Forgive yourself. You can't change what you did. You know, there are many people who wander around with tremendous feelings of guilt. Guilt and resentment are the most destructive emotions that anyone can experience.

I was raised with a lot of guilt. So as I got older, I was experiencing a lot of guilt, and I was having difficulty getting rid of it. Every little thing I did that I thought just wasn't quite right, I felt really guilty about. So I went to a psychiatrist in Southern California. I only went to that psychiatrist about four or five times. I was on my way there, and I decided I didn't have to go anymore. He was able to help me get rid of the guilt using the simple concept of forgiveness.

Forgiveness is a very healthy concept. We've got to learn to forgive ourselves. We've got to forgive others. We have to realize that we can't change what we did yesterday. Even if you did something deliberately wrong, let it go! And when it comes back into your mind, let it go again. If someone has done something to you, don't have any resentment, let it go. That doesn't mean you want to give them the opportunity to do it again. It's just that you simply can't hold bad thoughts in your mind and move in a good direction.

Forgiveness is one of the most liberating things you can ever do. Form the habit of not holding on to anything that is causing you to feel bad. Start loving yourself. Start respecting yourself. And have a healthy respect for what you are capable of doing.

Understand this: Carrying bad thoughts about anyone or anything is not doing anyone any good. It's sinful. It's destructive. And the price of sin is death. Now that doesn't mean they're going to bury you. But your bad thoughts may be burying your company. They may be burying your income. They may be burying your relationship or your friends.

Forgiveness will cause everything to grow. It will cause you to be healthier. It will cause your income to grow, your friends to grow, your business to grow. Just replace any thought of guilt or resentment with one of beauty, with one of plenty, with one of abundance.

Buckminster Fuller said, "You never change things by fighting the existing reality. To change something, build a new model that makes the existing model obsolete."

See yourself where you want to be and then be there. Don't be in the past. Be *there*! Act like the person you want to become.

CLASS TEN

# OUR MOST POWERFUL FORCE

*It Differentiates Us from
a Pig or a Horse*

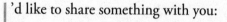

'd like to share something with you:

*Mind is the master power that moulds and makes,
And Man is Mind, and evermore he takes
The tool of Thought, and, shaping what he wills,
Brings forth a thousand joys, a thousand ills:—
He thinks in secret, and it comes to pass:
Environment is but his looking-glass.*

James Allen wrote those words a little over one hundred years ago. I began to study them about fifty-five years ago. Every year they mean a little more to me. These words describe the Law of Thinking.

Thinking is a powerful force. It has been said that it's the most powerful force we're capable of.

Archibald MacLeish, a Pulitzer Prize–winning playwright, wrote a play called *The Secret of Freedom*, and he had a character stand up and say, "The only thing about a man that is a man is his mind. Everything else you can find in a pig or a horse."

It's a funny line, but it's true. Everything else you can find in a pig or a horse. You see, thinking is a very, very powerful form of energy. Thought waves are cosmic waves that penetrate all time and space.

As we go into the Law of Thinking, I want to refer to several points Raymond Holliwell made in his fabulous book *Working with the Law*.

He said, "To the average person life is an enigma, a deep mystery, a complex and incomprehensible problem, or appears so, but it is very simple if one holds the key. Mystery is only another name for ignorance; all things are mysteries when they are not understood, but when we understand life, it no longer appears mysterious."

Until I was twenty-six, life was a real mystery to me. It was exactly how Holliwell described it: an incomprehensible problem. And I had a lot of problems! But then I began to study this information. It took me a while but as I started to adopt these concepts and adapt my mind to them, my life started to change. My problems started to disappear. I started to earn a lot more money. I was living in a healthy body, very rarely getting ill. I started to attract different people into my life, more interesting people. You see, the truth was that I was just becoming a more interesting person. A person is interesting because they're interested. You see, as we start thinking powerful thoughts, everything starts to change.

Raymond Holliwell also said:

*Man is a progressive being, a creature of constant growth, before whom lies an illimitable ocean of progress to be navigated and conquered only by development and culture of his inherent powers. The progress of the individual is largely determined by his ruling mental state, because the mind is the basic factor and governing power in the entire life of man. Attention should be given to the pre-dominant mental state, for it will regulate the action and direction of all one's forces, faculties and powers, the sum total of which will inevitably determine many particular experiences and the personal fate.*

You see, the ruling state is like the CPU in a computer. The central processing unit is the ruling state of the computer.

He continues:

*The ruling state of mind is made up of various mental attitudes which the individual adopts towards things, events, and life in general. If his attitudes are broad in mind, optimistic in tone, and true to life, his predominant mental state will correspond and exhibit a highly constructive and progressive tendency. As almost all the forces of the personality function through the conscious mind in one way or another, and as the daily mental and physical acts are largely controlled by the conscious mind, it is obvious that the leading mental state will determine the direction in which the powers of the individual are to proceed.*

The ruling mental state is so important—it really is everything. I know that you and I have been trained to believe that we've got to change what's going on out there. That we've got to fix this and fix that. We have literally been programmed to live through our senses— to go by what we see, hear, smell, taste or touch. But, as I previously brought to your attention, there has been little thought given to our higher faculties: our will, perception, imagination, intuition, memory and reason. Our inner faculties are where it really happens. It all begins inside.

You don't have to worry about changing what's going on out there. I don't care if it's your bank account or the health of your body. As you take over the power of thought, you're going to find that the X-rays will show a different you. The bank account will show a different balance. In fact, everything in life will begin to change.

Let me share what Raymond Holliwell said about thought:

> *Thought is a subtle element; although it is invisible to the physical sight, it is an actual force or substance, as real as electricity, light, heat, water or even stone. We are surrounded by a vast ocean of thought stuff through which our thoughts pass like currents of electricity, or tiny streaks of light or musical waves. You*

*can flash your thoughts from pole to pole, completely around the world many times in less than a single second. Scientists tell us that thought is compared with the speed of light. They tell us our thoughts travel at the rate of 186,000 miles per second. Our thought travels 930,000 times faster than the sound of our voice. No other force or power in the universe yet known is as great or as quick. It is a proven fact, scientifically, that the mind is a battery of force, the greatest of any known element.*

Isn't that amazing? You see, the thinker is like the computer processor. When it is finely tuned, it works really, really fast. You can think. And what you think ultimately produces the results in your life. It's a law.

I'm going to tell you something that I've learned beyond a shadow of a doubt. I have shared this with you before, but I want to reemphasize it. The thoughts that you think and turn over to your emotional mind instantly, by law, control the vibratory rate of your body. Your body is a mass of magnetic energy. It truly is. If you put your body in front of an infrared camera in a completely dark room, you'd just see it as a glistening, radiating form. And if you could hear your body, it would sound like a symphony.

Yet to the naked eye, it just looks like a thing. But it's not a thing. The body is one of the most magnificent instruments on the planet. You live in one. It's what you think that is going to dictate what your body is going to do. We know that our actions produce our results. If we want to change our results, we have to change our actions. However, if you don't go to the thought, the actions won't change. Well, they might change temporarily, but believe me, the thoughts that you think repeatedly become fixed in your subconscious mind. And those are the thoughts that are going to determine what happens in your life. Make no mistake about it.

Here's more from Holliwell:

*Some think that we must deal with two forces; that is, to attract the good we must do away with the bad, but this is not true. For example; if we are cold, we do not work with cold and heat alike in order to get warm. We build a fire, and as we gather around that fire we enjoy the heat that is extended from it and become warm. As we build up warmth, the cold disappears, for cold is the absence of heat. To be warm, we give our whole thought to those things which tend to create warmth; we ignore the cold in thinking of heat and bring forth heat. Prosperity and poverty are not two things; they are merely two sides of one and the same thing. They are but one power, rightly or wrongly used. We cannot think of plenty and then worry about the unfavorable conditions that may seem apparent. We think about plenty, and as we think of it, lack, its opposite, will become absorbed or disappear. All our thoughts must be directed to that one thing which we desire in order that our desire may be fulfilled. Our method is not manipulating two powers, not dealing with good and evil, right and wrong, prosperity and poverty, but as we follow the Law of Good and dwell upon that which is good we shall bring to pass all good things.*

If you want to change the results in your life, and I'm just working on the premise that you do, give some serious thought to how you're using your mind.

Aldous Huxley was right when he said, "There is only one corner of the universe you can be certain of improving, and that's your own self."

You know all those things we want to change outside, they're just a reflection of what is going on inside. That might be a big idea for you right now, but not when you study this for a week or a month. Everything you've heard about choosing your thoughts and your thoughts controlling your life is true. You become what you are thinking about. That is the Law of Thinking.

The way you are programmed genetically dictates whether you are going to operate predominately from the left or right hemisphere of your brain. The right hemisphere of the brain is the creative side. It deals with colors, pictures, music, feelings and so forth. The left hemisphere is more linear and analytical. It's more intellectual.

A person who is dominated by the left hemisphere is going to have a difficult time with this to start off with. First of all, we're raised to believe that's where your answers are. When we were little kids, they told us you've got to figure it out. We'd go to our parents and say, "I want this," and they'd respond, "Well, how are you going to get that?" The kid doesn't know how to get it. So we leave them with the impression that they can't get it because they can't figure out how to get it.

When they get older, they ask about something they really want to do. The parent says, "Where is the money going to come from?" Of course, they don't know. So they're left with the impression that they have to give up their dream. And they let it go. Unfortunately, that is programmed into their mind at a very early age. That's called environmental conditioning and it is rampant. If we want something, for example, and we can't see where the money is going to come from, we're programmed to believe that we should forget about it.

As a result, when most people think of a goal, if they can't see how it's going to happen, they won't set the goal. They keep backing up until they've got it all planned out and then say, "OK, I think I can do this."

Well, that's not setting a goal at all. That's aiming for something that you already know you can do. But there's no inspiration in going after something you think you can do. You've got to go after something you *want*.

Now, you may wonder why I say setting a goal that you know you can do isn't really setting a goal. I say that because you have to think about *why* you're setting the goal in the first place. Are you setting the goal to get the car, to get the house, to get the job? *No!* You're setting the goal to raise your conscious awareness. That's really the purpose of a goal. It's to bring more of you to the surface. And when you do, you enjoy everything you do more.

Setting a goal you can achieve is like dying. It's not inspiring. You won't get much support from others. You'll probably quit. But when you set a goal that inspires you, it doesn't matter if you don't get support. You're turned on; it sets something on fire inside of you. It's the way to live!

Now, understand that when you're going after what you want, you will not know how it's going to happen.

I've had the good fortune of working with Edmund Hillary (the first man to reach the top of Mount Everest) on three different occasions. The only thing that I could see different in Hillary than anyone else was his size. He's a big man. But he did not know how to get to the top of that mountain. He was a beekeeper from New Zealand. What did he know about getting to the top of the highest mountain in the world? Nobody had ever climbed that mountain. So he couldn't find out about it from someone else. He couldn't read about it. In fact, there was suffi-cient evidence to discourage 99 percent of the population from attempting it. Many people who had tried to climb that mountain had died. I am told you can find people encased in ice at the top. Their bodies are frozen there; they're never coming down.

Hillary was told he couldn't do it. In 1951, this bee-keeper got the money, his team and his guides together, and off they went. And they failed. They didn't get to the top of the mountain. They had to go home.

All his friends and relatives said, "I told you, you couldn't do it."

And he said, "Well, we didn't do it, but we're going to do it."

Then they started to get angry with him and said, "You're going to lose your life. The air is so thin up there you can't breathe. It's impossible to do."

But in 1952, he went back. More money. More resources. And he failed again. But you see, failing is part of winning. Failing just made him more determined.

So in 1953, he went back again. And this time he did it! He stood on top of Mount Everest.

Now more than one thousand people have climbed to the top of Mount Everest since Hillary did it. It's almost like people say: "If somebody has done it, then we believe it."

But Hillary believed it when nobody had ever done it. How did the Wright brothers get off the ground? You could prove that we couldn't fly. But they knew we could because they could see it.

If you can see it, then you can do it. How are you going to do it? Well, you'll be able to tell the person that *after* you do it. It's not all locked up in your intellect. It's locked up in faith. It's locked up in the belief that if you hold the idea in your mind, you'll move into the vibration that will attract it.

That's why you've got to understand the laws. You've got to understand your relationship to the laws. And you've got to know that you can do it. Where will the money come from? Wherever it is right now! You will attract it.

Hillary got to the top of the mountain because he believed he would get there! He understood how the mind worked. He understood that if he kept the image of what he *wanted* in his mind, he would succeed. He didn't see himself dying; he didn't see himself encased in ice forever. He saw himself going to the top and coming back down. And that's exactly what he did!

That's the way *you've* got to see it! You've got to see yourself getting to the top of *your* mountain. And know that everything you will need will come as you need it.

The only way you're really going to grasp this is to understand the Law of Thinking. You can't study this too much. I've been studying it every day now for over fifty-five years, and I think I'm really just getting a grip on it. But the beautiful part is, there's no end to it.

Think about this for a moment with respect to goals and goal achievement. You could be reading a good novel and you're really into it. You really don't want it to come to an end because you're enjoying it so much. Yet you do want it to come to an end, because you want to find out what happens. But you know it's going to come to an end. Or you could be out to dinner with someone and you're having a great time, but you know it's going to come to an end. You may be on vacation and you know it's coming to an end. Well, you may be locked into what I'm teaching and you know that this seminar is coming to an end. You know that.

But when you start studying yourself and your potential, there isn't any end to it. So for fifty-five-plus years I've woken up every day and I think, *I can get more. There's more. I can understand more.* It keeps you jazzed. It keeps you turned on. It winds your stem every day when you wake up, because you know you're dealing with the infinite.

Well, what are we talking about? We're talking about your potential. You don't know what you can do. Nobody knows what you can do. I don't care what you've done. Look at how I started out. I was unhappy. I was sick. I had only a couple of months of high school education. I was broke. I had no business experience. I mean, talk about losing. I was a real loser!

But all that stuff is in the past. It's behind you. That's where you've been. It doesn't have to determine where you're going to go. You're not going to figure out how to do it. Not until you've done it.

And here's another point. After you've done it, you still won't know how you did it because there are all kinds of little serendipitous things that happen while you're getting there that you are not even aware of.

I want you to imagine that you're working toward your goal. You know you're going to get there, but you don't know how. You've got this particular problem or challenge that is really stretching you. It is really testing you and you can't seem to solve it, but you're thinking about it all the time.

Now, you're shopping in the supermarket and there's

a long line to get to the cashier. So you're frustrated and all of a sudden somebody runs into your shopping cart. You turn around to see what happened and when you turn there's a headline on a tabloid that's in a rack. And whatever was in that headline hit your brain and triggered a series of thoughts and the solution to your problem pops into your mind.

After you reach the goal you look back, maybe three months later, and you think, *If that person hadn't run into my cart* . . .

That's one of those serendipitous things that happen to trigger your mind. Those things flip your mind onto a different frequency. You see, you think on frequencies. The answer to your problem is on a higher frequency than where the problem is. You've got to keep raising your level of conscious awareness.

Dr. Michael Beckwith said, "Consciousness is being aware that you are aware." That's such a beautiful way of putting it. Consciousness is being able to truly think about what you are thinking about.

# HOW TO TELL IF YOU'RE DOING IT WRONG

## *Living in Harmony with the Universal Laws*

L ook at what Thomas Edison said:

*I know the world is ruled by infinite intelligence. Everything that surrounds us, everything that exists, proves there are infinite laws behind it. There can be no denying this fact. It is mathematical in its precision.*

Everything operates by law. The law is exact. I see the law as God's modus operandi. It's how everything happens.

Wernher von Braun—I quoted him in the movie *The Secret*—he said the natural laws of the universe are so precise that we don't have any difficulty building space ships, we can send people to the moon and you can time the landing with the precision of a fraction of a second.

Our problem is, we see it, we believe it, von Braun said it, they use it, they go to the moon . . . but we don't bring it into our own life. We don't understand that thought is energy. We don't understand that thought waves are cosmic waves that penetrate all time and space. We don't understand that it's our thinking that controls the vibration of this body that we're living in. We don't understand that the vibration we're in dictates what we attract into our life. We don't understand that the same thing keeps reoccurring until we change the idea.

See, if you are in harmony with the law, your life is going to keep getting better. If you're living by the law, you're going to continue to earn more, you're going to feel better and you're going to have more fun. It just keeps getting better. And if it's not getting better, you're violating the law. It's that simple. Don't argue with it.

When I was a little boy, I went to Sunday school. I had to go to Sunday school or I'd get in trouble. When I'd play hooky, my sister would go home and tell my mother, and then I'd be in trouble, so I ended up going to Sunday school.

So I'm down there in the basement of the church with this introverted little girl who was a Sunday school teacher while the parents were upstairs singing and talking to one another. At any rate, I'm down there and I'm told that the price of sin is death. I always thought that was rather severe but they said it, so you know it must be the way it is. And then I was told if you do this, it's a sin, if you say that, it's a sin. I thought, *Golly, am I going to die?*

Well, I was pretty curious so I thought, *I'm going to try it.* I not only tried it, I did it, and I enjoyed it! I didn't die! And I did it again. I not only said it but it didn't hurt, you know, it felt good. And I thought, *I didn't die.*

I thought they meant that I'd literally die if I sinned, but you see, the problem was my perception of what was being said. My understanding was what was missing. Is the price of sin death? Yes. Absolutely. So you have to ask, well wait a minute—What is death?

Death is the opposite of life. If life is growth, then death must be ungrowth. *Ungrowth*—see, I'm going to be like Webster; I'm making up new words. I'll write a dictionary one day. Gina who has worked closely with me for over twenty-eight years says I spell them differently every time I spell. But at any rate, the basic law of life is to create or disintegrate. Disintegrate doesn't mean that you're just going to . . . *whoosh* . . . disappear. It means you're either going ahead or you're going back.

When you violate the law, that's a sin. Violate the law, you lose. Get in harmony with the law, you win. Make sense?

❖

Look at it this way—the law says give and you shall receive. When you hold out your hand to shake another person's hand, you don't ask for their hand, you just hold out your hand and you get one back. That's the way it works. When you do good, you get good. That's the law.

Now, if I go out and try and *get*, that's not going to work too well. If I'm out selling and I say, "I really want to help you," but I'm thinking, *I want some money, I hope*

*I make the sale*, I am violating the law. I'm sending the idea on a conscious level that *I want to help you*. So it's a positive idea intellectually, but emotionally—heart to heart—*I want your money*. So he's hearing the idea *I want to help you*, but the feeling he's picking up is *I want you to help me*. So what happens? I set up a conflict in his mind. Positive idea on a conscious level, negative idea in the subconscious. He doesn't understand what he's picking up emotionally, but he's still picking it up, and it still impacts him. To close a sale you've got to get the other party to write their name on a line. That's called orderly behavior. You're never going to get orderly behavior out of a mind that's in conflict.

But if I say, "I really want to help you," and I'm emotionally involved with wanting to help you, you know what you have to do, just like that. You don't have to worry about closing a sale. Closing a sale is a natural conclusion to a very fine presentation. You just want to fall in love with helping people. The amount of money you earn is always in direct relation to the amount of service that you render. This is all in harmony with the law.

❖

Wallace Wattles, the author of *The Science of Getting Rich*, devoted an entire chapter to the Law of Perpetual Increase. If you're going with the law, your results are going to keep getting better. Progress. Growth. When one good is realized, another desire for a greater good will develop. And then on to a higher state he's headed. You see, another and more glorious state will unfold. Your vision will urge you on and on. Hence, you'll discover the advancing life is the true life. The life that God intended you to live. It's supposed to keep getting better.

If your results aren't getting better, you're violating the law. You're going to lose. You're dying or your business is dying. That's the way it is. They may not be burying you, but your sales are going down, you're earning less money, you don't feel as good, you haven't got any energy, you're just sort of spent.

That should be a warning sign. You should think, *Wait a minute, what happened to me?* I must be violating the law. Just think of helping people. Get a big idea in your mind. Start to create. Feel good.

When I was a little boy my grandmother pretty much raised me. We always thought Grandma was like God. She was a dear little lady but she didn't have the right ideas. Grandma used to say, "You should be satisfied with what you've got, dear." Grandma was wrong!! You should be happy with what you've got, but you should never be satisfied.

Dissatisfaction is a creative state. See, dissatisfaction is what keeps us reaching. What does the law say? It says bigger, better, faster. That's why the runners want to run faster. Jumpers want to jump higher. Singers want to sing more. People who are earning money want to earn more. You want to do more. Is it to get it? No! It's to grow. Goals are not to get stuff. Goals are to grow. Getting is nice, but a side benefit is that the bigger the goal, the more alive you're going to become. It's pretty basic.

You are a spiritual being. You live in a physical body. But the physical is just the physical manifestation of a higher side of you.

Where is spirit? Spirit is omnipresent. Well, what does that mean? Spirit is everywhere. Spirit is in this lectern here. Spirit's in the platform, it's in the computer, it's in the air.

You say, now it's really getting confusing. You'll say spirit is not in the garden rock. Well, wait a minute—spirit's everywhere except in a garden rock! Huh. Well, is spirit in a tree? Spirit's omnipresent except in a garden rock or a tree! Hmmm. Is spirit in the tire on my car? No! No! Not in the tire of a car! It's spirit! Spirit's everywhere except in a garden rock, a tree and the tires in my car! Wait a minute—if it is everywhere, it's everywhere.

Do you see how people get confused? You know what we should do: We should think of something else. But instead we think, *Let's turn the television on. Get lost in somebody else's world.* That's what we do.

The tire of the car is made of the same stuff your body is made of. The tree is made of the same stuff your body's made of. The garden rock is made out of the same stuff your body is made of.

The garden rock is moving. Everything moves. We live in an ocean of motion. Nothing rests. That wall is moving. It appears to be still but it's really not. A body in a coffin is moving. There's no such thing as dead. That's a false concept. The body in a coffin is moving. If the body isn't moving, how would it ever change to dust? See, if you picked up the remains and looked at it through a microscope, you'd see it moving. Dancing right before your eyes. And it will turn to dust. Why? Because it moves. Everything moves. Nothing rests. Nothing is either created or destroyed; that just postulates the theory of life. There is no such thing as death. You moved into your body and you will move out of your body. Both life and death are transitions and parts of the same great adventure.

Do you want to know the difference between us and other creatures on Earth? We're creative beings. We're created in the image of God. We can cause spirit to move in the way that we want. We can cause it to move into whatever form we want.

But do you know what happened? We got the equation reversed. We created God in our image and now we're trying to figure out how He—*He*, not She—can be omnipresent. Can you see where this goes? It goes down the wrong path. Why? Because we're ignorant. We just don't understand. But if we study—everything you study in your religion, you're going to find that it's true. It's our *perception* that we have a problem with. You and I are spiritual beings. We live in a physical body. But unlike the rest of the animal kingdom, we were given an intellect. We were given intellectual faculties that no other form of life has. It's how we use these intellectual faculties that dictates our emotional state.

What is the emotional state? It's how we feel. It's the vibration we're in. So when we talk about the vibration we're in—we're talking about our emotional state. Feeling is conscious awareness of the vibration we're in. When you say you're not feeling good, what you're really saying is "I am consciously aware that I'm not in a good vibration."

"What's the matter?"

"I'm just feeling so bad."

"Why?"

"Well, it's the way he's acting." Ohhhh. You're letting his actions control your feelings. Why would you let his actions control your feelings?

"Well, you don't know what it's like. If you knew the financial problems I have, you'd know why I'm upset."

Why would you get upset over finances? What is the point in that? Why would you get upset over anything? Why don't you just look at it—it is what it is, accept it. It's either going to control you or you're going to control it.

Here's something everyone really needs to understand. You know, I know people and you know people who are working on personal development. They've got a great library of material, they've attended a bunch of seminars, but they really don't make it happen. And where they're puzzled is "How do I earn some money?"

How many people are puzzled by that? Be honest. Hold your hand way up. Stand up. Quite a few of you. Thank you. I do that so you can acknowledge it to yourself.

In *Think and Grow Rich*, Napoleon Hill says:

*If you're one of those who believe that hard work and honesty alone will bring riches, perish the thought! It is not true! Riches, when they come in huge quantities, are never the result of hard work alone! Riches come in response to definite demands based upon the application of definite principles. Not by chance or luck.*

Who are you going to demand it of? Are you going to demand it of God? Are you going to demand it of somebody else?

The quote says, "Riches come in response to definite demands based upon the application of definite principles. Not by chance or luck." So the demand would have to be on yourself. You've got to *demand* it of yourself. And then, you've got to follow the rules. You've got to work with the law.

You could very easily just skip over that, but there is an absolute Law of Compensation.

We give out a card in our seminars at some point where we quote Don Shula, the great American football coach. He said, "The start is what stops most people."

This is not rocket science. This is getting really honest with yourself. Most people do not demand it of themselves. You've got to demand it. You've got to really apply this.

The Law of Compensation clearly states that the amount of money you earn will always—not some of the time, not only in Russia or the United States—*always*, in all places at all times, be in exact ratio to these three points: (1) the need for what you do, (2) your ability to do it, and (3) the difficulty there will be in replacing you.

I believe that what we do at PGI is in very high demand all over the world. I have $40 on me. You could put me on a plane to anywhere in the world with just this

$40, and I guarantee you that I would immediately start multiplying it. Immediately.

Because I know that what I know how to do is in demand everywhere in the world. I have never gone anywhere in the world where it wasn't in demand.

We went into Shanghai and they had to get about twenty people to hold hands around us because people were trying to get at me. They knew I had something they wanted. I guess they thought if they got close enough, they would get it. That's not how you get it. The bottom line is that you've already got it!

You can always tell a person's level of understanding by their results. If the results aren't there, they don't know it's because they're not living in harmony with the law. I don't care what kind of story they give you. They don't know! And unfortunately, in most cases, they don't know that they don't know.

This is something every person in this room is interested in. The amount of money you earn is in exact ratio to the need for what you do.

I didn't know that when I got into this business. I didn't get into this business because of that. I got into this business because I absolutely loved it. I just could not get enough and I still can't get enough! It's like I've been hungry for this since the first day I heard a record. I *never* heard anyone talking like Earl Nightingale on that record.

You see, I know there's no limit on the amount that I can earn. And I know that the only way to raise my income is to understand this better. The trick isn't in the marketing. The trick isn't in your sales presentation. The trick is in your understanding. If the understanding isn't there, you're not going to earn more money.

That's why Solomon said, "With all thy getting get understanding." There's only one way to get understanding. One way, not two. Just one. And that's through study. There is no other way.

There are many forms of study, but you've got to study! Knowledge is omnipresent. All the knowledge there ever was or ever will be is everywhere all the time. It's in all places at the same time.

Your computer has always been here. It didn't just arrive with Steve Jobs or Bill Gates. It has *always* been here! We were just not aware of it. Edison became aware that there was magic in the air and that he could bottle it, direct it, and harness it. Niagara Falls has been there for a *lo-o-o-ng* time. It had to be channeled to provide all of the power generated by the Falls.

You've got to understand it. The amount of money

you earn is in exact ratio to the need for what you do. I see people who come back here over and over. They make a little progress and they think they've got it. And I don't think we ever get it. I think we're always getting it.

At age eighty-seven, Michelangelo said, "I am still learning." You've got to keep learning.

Our educational system and corporate training programs are incomplete. There's something missing. I say that because 3 percent of the population is earning 97 percent of the money. Something is wrong! That's why I know there will always be a very high demand for what I do.

I have an opinion, and I don't think I'll ever get shaken off this. I believe if a program you're studying doesn't have a spiritual foundation, it is incomplete. If it's incomplete, you're not going to win.

I don't teach religion. I'm not qualified to teach religion, but I do know something about the spiritual side of our life. I do know this: Your essence is spirit, and spirit is always for expansion. It is never for disintegration. It is always for growth, always. Something in you wants to grow.

So whatever you're doing you're going to want to do it better. If you're running, you're going to want to run faster. If you sing, you want to sing better. If you sell, you want to sell more. If you jump, you want to jump higher. It's in your nature to grow and expand.

⋄⋄⋄

The second part of the Law of Compensation is that the amount of money you earn will always be in exact ratio to your ability to do it.

I've become very good at this, but I know I can get a whole lot better. And because I'm very good, I'm difficult to replace, which is the third part of the law. But I *can* be replaced. There's no such thing as being indispensable.

There is a great poem called "The Indispensable Man" by Saxon White Kessinger. It says:

> *Take a bucket and fill it with water,*
> *Put your hand in it up to the wrist,*
> *Pull it out and the hole that's remaining,*
> *Is a measure of how much you'll be missed.*
> *You can splash all you wish when you enter,*
> *You may stir up the water galore,*

*But stop, and you'll find that in no time,*
*It looks quite the same as before.*

Now, what I'm doing is getting the idea across that no one is indispensable. If you start to get the idea that you are indispensable, your ego is taking over and you're really screwed. You're going in the wrong direction.

These are the basics. We've got to understand where the power is. The power is in the spiritual essence of who you are. And as long as you recognize that, study that and start being a better instrument for it to flow through, your results are going to improve. You've got to get better at what you're doing.

Napoleon Hill said, "Do not go searching for opportunity but reach out and embrace it right where you are."

Well, if you go back and think about it for a moment, if the need is there, and you're difficult to replace because you're good enough, the trick is to keep getting better. So the only part of the Law of Compensation that you really have to focus on is the second one—focus on your ability to do the work. Just keep getting better at what you do. And understand that you can always get better.

We see that every day. Where it's really evident is in sports. The records continue to get shattered. You know, for years they used to think man couldn't run a mile faster. They used to let wild animals chase them and they couldn't run it any faster. Roger Bannister broke it into small parts and he broke the four-minute mile. But within a month, somebody else broke his record. And now, if you look at the Boston Marathon, they're nearly running a four-minute mile in a marathon. They're running a five-minute mile and doing it twenty-six times! You couldn't conceive of anything like that not too long ago.

# THE ONLY LIMIT ON POWER

## *Tapping into the Abundance of the Universe*

You've got to understand that the universe is abundant. My goodness. You can go right back to the Upanishads, the most ancient writing there is. It says, "From abundance he took abundance, and still abundance remains."

You say, "Well, how do you do that?"

Take a deep breath. Come on, suck it all in. Come on.

Hold it. Just stay like that for the rest of the day. You see, you wouldn't think of doing that.

From abundance he took abundance, and still abundance remains.

You say, "That's different." No, it isn't. It's exactly the same.

We've got to understand that everything operates by the same law. All success in life is due to taking sides with the law within us. OK. Thus, working with the law may be considered the same as taking the law into our lives and mind as a silent partner.

You could be taking the law into your own hands—working in harmony with the law.

It makes sense, doesn't it? How do you go ahead? Well, you've got to see yourself there first. You've got to act like you're already there.

Where does it happen? It happens intellectually. If I've got an idea in my consciousness, then I can share the idea with you and your consciousness, can't I? If I've got it, then I can give it to you. Does that make sense? I don't have to get it if I've got it. If I've got it, I've got it. And if I've got it, I can talk to you about it, can't I?

So if I've got an idea intellectually, I can share it with you intellectually. My intellect could share it with your intellect on a conscious level. I don't have to have it here on the physical plane. I could talk to you about all kinds of money. So I'm not getting it, I've got it. If I get emotionally involved with the idea, I could share those emotions with you. If I've got it intellectually and emotionally, then I've got it. Is that right?

Sixty-seven years before the life of Christ, Horace said, *"Nemo dat quod non habet."* Freely translated that means "You cannot give what you haven't got." But the opposite of that is that you can give what you've got. If I've got it intellectually, I can share it with you intellectually. If I've got it emotionally, I can share it with you emotionally. The only thing I can't do is enjoy it on the physical or share it with you on the physical.

You see, that's where the problem is. We live through our physical senses. If it isn't there on the physical, you say, "Well, I haven't got it!" Oh yes I have. I can talk to you about it. I can feel it. I can share my feelings with you. It's just that it hasn't manifested in form yet. Where does it come from?

Everything comes from the nonphysical. You work from a higher to a lower potential. Who's an engineer? Do we have an electrical engineer here? There's got to be one. Admit it. Is there one? All right.

If I'm working with electricity, I've got to work from a higher to a lower potential, don't I? If I try to go contrary to that, I'm going to be in trouble. Wouldn't you agree? The only limit on electricity is the limit that is placed on the form through which it flows. (*Pointing to a light.*) We call that electricity, but it's really not. It's an expression of electricity, isn't it? Well, the only limit on electricity is the limit on the form through which it's flowing. A seventy-five-watt bulb has more power than a sixty-watt bulb. And a one-hundred-watt bulb has even more power, correct?

Well, the only limit on *spiritual* power is the form through which it's flowing: *you*. Build a bigger idea and you'll experience a greater expression of the power. So you see a person walking around, no juice, no energy, they haven't got a very big idea. All you have to do is watch a person and that will tell you what's going on in their mind. Because the body is the instrument of the mind. The body expresses what's going on. When you see a person and they're lethargic and dragging themselves around, you know that they're bored. You know that they haven't got anything but bad ideas—if they're thinking anything at all!

Most people aren't even thinking. They're just a

plaything for what's going on around them. They're like a cork in the ocean, bouncing all over the place. A person who is thinking knows exactly where they're going. They're using their higher faculties: their reason, will, intuition, perception, memory and imagination.

Look at *spirit*—where is spirit? Spirit is omnipresent. Look at the lines on a lined sheet of paper and let those lines represent levels of vibration, more commonly referred to as frequencies. Everything operates by law and one of the laws is the Law of Vibration. OK. Now where is spirit? Spirit is everywhere. It is everything. It is the highest part of our personality. What's the lowest? The physical. Now what's right in the middle? The intellect. That's what makes us different from any other form of life. It's through the intellect that we can tap in on a higher level and change things on a lower level.

Here's what we've got to understand—you let this sink in and you're going to realize that everything is connected. Like the colors of a rainbow—each frequency is hooked up to the one above and the one below. There is no line of demarcation. You're hooked into everything in the universe. Everything. You're hooked into it. Your marvelous mind can tap in to the higher level—the spiritual. Every line on the page is connected to the one above and the one below. Focus on the nonphysical—see what you want. See yourself with it.

But we don't do that, do we? We go to the lowest level. We look at the bank account to see where we are financially. We go to the computer to see what our results are. You see. Well, what are you doing that for? Everybody does it. They teach you to do it. That's how you know where you're at. Ohhh. I wonder if they're all wrong. You say, "Well, they can't all be wrong." Why? They always have been!

When you see a large group of people going one way and only a few going the other way, follow the small group. You'll probably never make another mistake as long as you live. If you follow the masses, you're really going to be in a mess. Why? Because the masses have no idea where they're going. They've got to wait to turn on the news to see what kind of day it is. They look out the window and say, "Oh my, well this is going to be a bad day for traffic." Why not look at it differently? "Well, we won't have to drive as fast, we can go slower you know, it will give us an opportunity to think. We can enjoy our drive." That's a pretty silly way to think though, isn't it? Let's do what we always do and get upset. Yeah, let's get in the car and get upset. Go fast, then slow. Slam right into the jerk. Get the car all smashed up. You know.

You say, "Wait a minute—if it's this simple, why isn't everybody doing it?" That's a pretty good question. Let's look at this a different way.

# DANCE 'TIL IT RAINS

*Transforming Your Thoughts into Things*

W hy don't you act like the person you want to become? Why don't you act like the star who you really are? You know why you don't? Because you're afraid of what *they* think.

You know when that started? When you were just a little kid. They said, "What would the neighbors think?" Who cares?! I found out what the neighbors think—they don't! Quit concerning yourself with what the neighbors think! Act like the person you want to become.

*You are the offspring of a deathless soul.* This is what you want to burn into your mind! There's a power that's all knowing, that's ever present. That's what you're an expression of. It's so important that you get this straight, *so* important. Where do you really want to go?

Ralph Waldo Emerson said, "There is no planet, sun, or star could hold you, if you but knew what you are." Sear that into your mind.

⁘

It's what we feed into our subconscious mind, which is also the emotional mind, that dictates the vibration that the body moves into. The body being the instrument of the mind, the vibration dictates what you attract into your life. If you operate with a big idea—you see yourself operating with a very successful business and you see your things really flying—do you know what you're going to do? If you keep that picture, you're going to attract people who will make that happen.

But if you let the business control you and you complain about this person and that person and how bad things are, you're going to repel anybody who's got any speed on them at all, and you're going to attract more problems.

So see what you want. Hold the image of yourself already there. Change your vibration.

There's a cute story about a tribe in Africa. They have a rain dance. A lot of tribes in Africa have rain dances, but this tribe is different. Every time they dance, it rains!

Anthropologists have gone to study these people because it doesn't rain every time most tribes do a dance. So they went and studied this one tribe to find out why it rains every time they dance.

Do you want to know what they found out? They found out the tribe dances *until* it rains. *Ahhh.*

Every time I go out, I make a sale. How? Because I stay out until I make the sale! *Ahhh.*

This is not rocket science. It's simple stuff.

Let's get a glass, OK? Let's put water in the glass. Where did the water come from? It came from *nothing*, from spirit. What is the water made of? The water is energy. What's the glass made of? Energy. The glass used to be sand. What we did was change the vibratory rate of the energy that we called sand, and we turned it into glass.

So now we've got a sand full of water? Well, no. We call it glass now. We have a glass full of water. It's not a sand full of water. It's a glass full of water. It's energy full of water. We call the energy sand . . . no, we call it glass. Where does the water go? If you add heat to the water, it turns into steam, and the steam turns into air, ether or gas.

Here's what we want to grasp: There's no line of demarcation where it stops becoming one and starts to become the other. There's no line of demarcation where it stops becoming water and starts becoming steam. It's all hooked together.

If you make this simple enough, you can't miss it. You see, they're all frequencies. Just different frequencies. We call it steam because it's on a different frequency. Now stay with me. Where does it come from? Well, we bring it back—it comes from ether to the steam to the water, but get this, every line is hooked up to the one above and the one below.

You say, "Where are you going with this?" Where do you want me to go? I know where we'll go. Let's go to our thinking.

Here we are—there's spirit. We've got spirit. We've got the intellect and, voila, we've got the physical. Now let's activate our intellectual faculties. Do you know what your intellectual faculties are? We touched on them before. One of them is reason. That gives us the ability to think. So let's activate our reasoning factor and let's tap in on a higher level. Where's thought? Thought is omnipresent. Where's spirit? It's omnipresent. So we tap into our spiritual essence, pull our thoughts together and we build an idea.

This hotel was nothing but an idea at one time. We hold an idea long enough and the idea will move into form. That's what Andrew Carnegie said: "Any idea that is held in the mind, that is emphasized, that is either feared or revered, will begin at once to clothe itself in the most convenient and appropriate form available." If you hold the idea, it will move into form. See, all we're doing is working with the law. We're working with energy. We're working with the power. We're working with spirit.

We have the ability to be, do or have whatever we want. I don't care what your past is. Did you have some traumatic experience? It doesn't matter. Let it go! Tune in at the subconscious level. Say, "Wow, I am surrounded by power! It's flowing to and through me! Wow!"

This is cool. I can *think*! Thank you, God! I can *think*! I *think* I'm rich! I got rich. I *think* I'm happy. How do you become happy? Help others be happy. How do you become loved? Love others. This is pretty simple. I mean, I learned it!

QUESTION: I have a question—How can I attract the perfect idea to myself from spirit?

BOB: Well, the "perfect idea" is the idea that you're in love with.

If you love someone, you've attracted the perfect person, haven't you? Does that make sense? But someone else says, "You love that turkey? What's the matter with you?" So it's a matter of perception then. The perfect idea is the idea that you're emotionally involved in.

Do you know what love is? Love is resonance. It's when the conscious, subconscious and body are all in love with one idea. It's also called integrity. Your thoughts, feelings and actions are all lined up. So you just have to ask yourself, "What do I really love doing?"

# THE ONLY SOURCE
# OF SUPPLY

*Discover All the Secrets of Success*

Do you know what prayer is? I'm going to tell you what it is. It's not getting on your knees and saying, "God help me." That's making a noise on your knees. Prayer is the movement that takes place between spirit and form with and through us. We tap into the nonphysical and we create the physical.

You don't have to wonder where it's going to come from. There's only one source. There's one source of supply. If you think other people are your source, you're probably going to slow down. But then you realize there's only one source of supply: infinite. I call that source God, you call it whatever you want—call it intelligence, universal intelligence, Allah—you raise your level of consciousness until you are one with it. Then you just perform the magic.

There is one power. Every religion that has maintained its balance over any period of time has done so based on the emotional appeal of a future promise that you will one day become one with your God. You could part the seas, you could do whatever, because you're working in harmony with the law.

People come to my classes from all over the world. They come from Israel, South America, Australia, from all over Europe and all over North America. People travel all that distance. You know why? They want more of this. Why do they want more of it? Because it's in harmonious vibration with the essence of who they are.

In *Working with the Law*, Raymond Holliwell says:

> *All of the processes of nature are successful. Nature knows no failures. She never plans anything but success. She*

*aims at results in every form and manner. To succeed in the best and fullest sense of the term we must, with Nature as our model, copy her methods. In her principles and laws we shall discover all the secrets of success.*

Keep in mind, everything in this universe that you can see with the naked eye, and everything you cannot see, is an expression of spirit. Also bear in mind that spirit operates by exact laws. You are subject to those laws in just the same manner as nature is. Therefore, Holliwell is right—we definitely should copy nature's methods.

You see, this is an orderly universe. Nothing happens by accident. The images you plant in your marvelous mind instantly set up an attractive force that governs your results in life. You must remember, though, that this process is equally as effective with positive images as it is with negative ones.

Although it is true that everything you will ever want is already here—if not in form, in substance—it is up to you to get into harmony with it. Since you do attract everything into your life by law, it would be a wise move on your part to begin forming the habit of thinking only of what you want, regardless of the conditions or circumstances you may presently find yourself facing.

# THE MAGIC GRAPHIC

## *Mapping Your Mind*

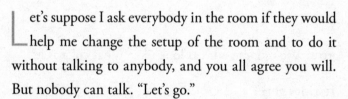

Let's suppose I ask everybody in the room if they would help me change the setup of the room and to do it without talking to anybody, and you all agree you will. But nobody can talk. "Let's go."

Finally somebody would say, "What does he want us to do?"

You'd say, "I don't know, ask him." "Why don't you ask him?!" "I can't talk."

You know we'd have chaos in here. Do you know why? Because nobody's got a picture. There's no picture. But out of confusion comes order and it's a higher degree of order than that which existed prior to the confusion. So now I say, "I'm going to make that the front of the room, and that the back of the room." (*pointing*) In a few seconds flat we'd have order, wouldn't we? Why? Because everybody's operating with the same picture.

Do you realize we've got people going to work and they have no picture? They don't even know what they're working for. They don't know which way to go. They don't know if they should talk to anybody. Maybe they should turn on the television and get lost in somebody else's world until they get this figured out. So they watch *The Price Is Right* for a little while. Their mind is in a total state of confusion. You have got to have order.

**BOB:** What does your car look like? What color is it?

**JIM:** It's gray.

**BOB:** What color is your refrigerator?

**JIM:** It's silver.

**BOB:** What color is your mind?

**JIM:** Lots of colors.

**BOB:** Hmmm. Is it big or small?

**JIM:** Sometimes it's big and sometimes it's small.

**BOB:** Is *yours* big? Is it bigger than a bread box?

**KAREN:** Yes.

**BOB:** It is. What color is it?

**KAREN:** All colors.

**BOB:** How big is it?

**KAREN:** Big.

**BOB:** How big is that?

You see . . . we're getting into a problem here, aren't we? That's because nobody's ever seen the mind. You start talking about the mind and there's no image.

Dr. Thurman Fleet in San Antonio, Texas, understood this back in 1934, and he decided he was going to give order to the mind. So he created a graphic illustration of the mind. He said, "We've never seen the mind. Let this represent the mind. And there's the body."

This is the basic graphic:

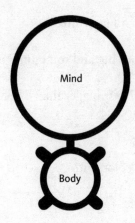

Now that is a genie. That is the most valuable graphic I have ever seen.

Let's take more detailed a look at the genie using the following graphic:

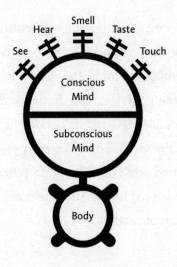

Here we have the mind and the body, but we've divided the graphic of the mind into two parts: the conscious mind and the subconscious mind.

We have sensory factors—we can see, hear, smell, taste and touch. And we have been programmed to live through these senses. As little kids, people will say—"Would you listen to what I'm telling you?" "Will you look at this?" "Will you listen to what I'm saying?" They're like little antennae. We become the plaything for everything that's going on outside. We let the bank account, what people say, what we think people think and our perception of what they think of us control us. We use our sensory factors—it's all outside input.

What we want to understand is that those sensory factors get us into a lot of trouble. They are given to us to help us communicate and correspond with our outside world. We are not meant to let them control our life. We don't want to become subjective to what's going on around us.

Now let's grasp this concept. The conscious mind is also what we call the intellectual mind. Let's take a look again at our intellectual factors (see the graphic below):

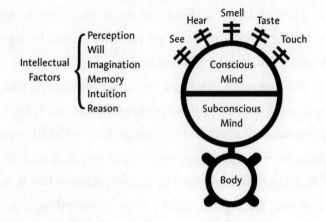

You have **perception**. Perception is an intellectual factor. We know the world is round. At one point we thought it was flat. What did we change? We changed our perception. The world didn't change. The world is the same as it was then. It was always round. It was our perception of it that changed.

My perception of the world—my world that I lived in—and my ability to earn money, is what changed for me. I always had the ability to earn money even when I was struggling and wasn't earning any. Why wasn't I earning any money? Because I thought I couldn't earn any. See, the truth was that I wasn't thinking. I was letting the outside world control me. Your perception is your reality. You can change the perception of the business you're in. Change your perception of how you operate your business.

You and I were talking about that, Dan. I was firing some things back at you and I said change your perception of what you're doing, and you would probably make more headway, wouldn't you? And you'd make a lot more money.

The **will** is another intellectual faculty. Bruce came to a seminar. I said, "Turn your annual income into a monthly income." He's the principal of a school. So what did he do? He turned his annual income into his monthly income. He shocked himself with what he could earn. You'll be amazed at what you can do when you have the will.

When Dr. Wernher von Braun was asked by President Kennedy what it would take to build a rocket to take a man to the moon, he answered with just five words. He didn't say you're going to have to get all the top scientists in the world together and really brainstorm and . . . he didn't say any of that. When he answered Kennedy, he answered him in these five words: "The will to do it."

What do you need to get to where you want to go? Well, first of all, where do you want to go? You need the will to do it. Do you know where you want to go, Linda? Are you sure? You do know? That's all you need is the will to do it. Do you know where you want to go, Michelle? You do know. That's all you need: the will to do it. Do you know where you want to go, Mike? You don't know where you want to go. Well, you're probably not going to go anywhere then. But that's what it takes.

What is the will? The will is a mental faculty that gives you the ability to focus. You take this power that's flowing into your consciousness—if you could see it, it would be like a funnel flowing right into the crown of your head. And as it flows into your consciousness, you have the ability to turn it into a picture.

Let's think about it for a minute. Let's suppose that I get up and hang a sign on that wall and I turn out all the lights and then I light a candle. With the candlelight I'm trying to read the sign on that wall. But I can't read it. It's not that there's not enough candle power. There is. It's just that it's not being directed to the picture. Some of it is going there (*pointing*), some of it is coming on me. Some of it is going up there, down there, over there.

Well, if I took the same candle power and I put it in a flashlight, none of it would be wasted. I'd marshal that energy and I'd focus it on one spot. That's what happens with your mind when you marshal the energy that's flowing into your consciousness. The will gives you the ability to focus on one image to the exclusion of all outside distractions.

If I'm standing behind you in a mall and I'm staring at you, you'll feel it, won't you? You will feel it. If my staring is really strong, you're *really* going to feel it. You'll get a very uncomfortable feeling. What's happening? I am staring at you. I've got one idea—it's you—on the screen of my mind. I'm sending that energy—it's just rifle-firing right into your brain. I'm sending cells right into your brain. It's causing an uncomfortable feeling. You'll turn around and you'll see me, and I'll turn away. Feeling is conscious awareness of vibration.

Do you know what the picture or image you've created in your mind does? It marshals the energy. It increases the amplitude of vibration, and the energy flow coming from you is increased dramatically. It becomes much more powerful.

The will to do it. That's what got us to the moon. That's what got us to do everything we're doing. The will gives you power.

Then you've got your imagination. Your marvelous imagination. It's absolutely criminal the way we've treated our imagination and the way we were taught to do it. Why do we have great big corporations and weak little creative departments? Why do we sit there and talk about why we can't do something when all we have to do is totally relax, let our imagination go, see ourselves doing it and Wow, I can see it!! I can see that great big company. I can see us operating all over the world.

I sat in a room—in a little room—in a house on Maplewood Lane in Glenview, Illinois, and I took my pen and I wrote down "I'm going to have a company that'll operate all over the world," and now I have a company that operates all over the world. I think we operate in ninety-some countries right now. Now I want to do $100 million. I want to expand what I'm doing. I want to do it in a bigger way. Why? Because I want to. Because I want to. That's all you have to know. I just want to.

You're thinking, *Well, there must be some reason why you want to.* Yeah. I want to. That's why. I just want to. *Well, what are you going to do with the money?* I don't know. Maybe give it away. It doesn't matter what I do with it. See, we'll do something with it and we'll try and do it constructively. We certainly don't want to just sit and count it all the time—pile it up and oh, look at all the money! *What do you want to do that for?* It's an instrument that we put to work. We want to put it to work doing something that we'd have fun doing. That's constructive. Something that serves us and serves others.

"You see, the imagination," Hill said, "is the most marvelous, miraculous, inconceivably powerful force the world has ever known. You can build castles in your mind."

Way back in 1970, I worked for Kemmons Wilson and Wallace Johnson at the Holiday Inn Memphis–University of Memphis, Tennessee. In 1950 there wasn't one Holiday Inn. In 1970 there were more Holiday Inns than the Hilton, Ramada and Sheraton chains combined. They were building a new room every thirteen minutes! Do you know why? Wilson had gone on a vacation with his family, and he was appalled at the state of the hotels on the road, at what it cost them for kids. He discussed it with Johnson and they thought, *Why doesn't somebody build a fine chain of hotels and let the kids stay for nothing?* And that's exactly what they decided to do. That's where the Holiday Inns came from.

Kemmons Wilson and Wallace Johnson built those. Then they sold out to the Bass Corporation and Wallace Johnson died. Kemmons Wilson at eighty was bored. He started to build the Wilson Inns, and before he died he built one hundred of them. He also wrote a book: *Half Luck and Half Brains*. I've got an autographed book from him.

Age has nothing to do with it! It's your thinking that has everything to do with it. It's how you use your imagination. Where did we get the idea that age made a difference or gender could make a difference? Why does a woman earn 70 percent of what a man earns? Who thought of that idea? What validity is there to it? There's none! But you know something, if you and I graduated as electrical engineers and we both went out and got a job right here in this city today, I would earn more than you in almost all companies. Why? Because I'm a man. You'll say, "Well, that's not right." It doesn't matter whether it's right or not, that's what they do. I don't know why every woman doesn't go into business for herself and fire all the men. Women literally run our company. They literally run the company. We didn't just hire women to run the company. They just happen to run the company.

Think! You can do anything you want. You can do whatever you want. It's the imagination. Use the imagination. Understand that that's where everything starts for you. But when you get the picture in the imagination, don't let it go, and say, "Ahhh, that was nice. Yeah, I really enjoyed doing that, but it's just an idea." What are you talking about? It's direction for your life. It's inspiration for you. It'll keep you alive. It will give you juice all the days of your life.

Everybody's got a perfect memory. If we have time, I'll get you to demonstrate that. I could show you how to remember a hundred things just like that. Jerry Lucas was teaching people to memorize the Bible in San Francisco a number of years ago. We had a psychiatrist, Abdullah, in from Saudi Arabia, and he was teaching people how to memorize the Koran. Most people can't remember their phone number. We have a perfect memory.

Then you have **intuition.** We were talking and I was telling Andy what he was like, and I wasn't just fairly accurate, I was very accurate, wasn't I? Yes. You see. And he's saying, "Well, how do you do that?" You become aware . . . it's your intuitive factor, you pick it up and you read it. You're going to find that good police officers are very intuitive. Good customs agents are intuitive. I remember there was a customs agent at the Toronto airport. Stringer was his last name, Jim Stringer. I got to know him while going through the airport. I got to know the guys in customs by their first names. Then I saw in the paper that Jim had died. He was a fairly young man; he was only in his forties. I remember I got his address, and I sent a card to his wife because I really liked the guy. We used to stop and talk a lot and something I didn't know about him is that he was one of the top agents out here at the airport. He picked out more people smuggling drugs into the country and different things than anybody else there. It was his intuition. They wrote about it in the newspaper and said he was a very intuitive person. He just sensed that you were breaking the law, and it turned out he was right.

Your intuition is one of your faculties. It's a higher faculty and it's in your conscious mind. It enables you to tune in to life on a subconscious, universal level. It enables you to pick up other people's energy and translate it, so you know what they're thinking. You don't have to be with them, because this is not physical. They could be on the other side of the globe and you will still pick up their energy. You will feel it. It's your intuitive factor that does that. It translates the energy that you pick up so you can know what's going on.

Then of course you have **reason**. That's what gives you the ability to think.

Your **imagination** is a powerful mental faculty. Imagination is the mental faculty out of which visions arise. It deals with the *might be* element in your life. Your imagination allows you to go into the future and bring the future back into the present and act like the person you want to become. Napoleon Hill described the imagination as "the most marvelous, miraculous, inconceivably powerful force the world has ever known." And you own it. Imagination gave us the electric light, the ball point pen, air travel, the computer chip; everything you see that was made by man was first originated in someone's imagination.

And then we have the **memory**. There's no such thing as a bad memory. There are only weak memories. Memory is a mental muscle that can be strengthened in exactly the same manner physical muscles are strengthened—through repetitious, perfect practice. Most people say practice makes perfect. The truth is perfect practice makes perfect.

You can use all six of those higher mental faculties (will, perception, intuition, memory, imagination and reason) to create magic in your mind. In fact, our institute built a program on the development of your higher faculties, and it is called "The Magic in Your Mind."

Let's take a look at the following graphic:

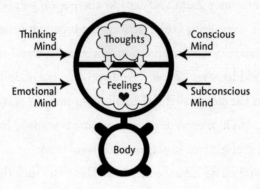

You see, you've got the conscious mind, the subconscious mind and the body. The conscious mind is your thinking mind. That's where your thoughts are formed— you can entertain thoughts there. The subconscious is the emotional mind.

So you build ideas and your dream in your conscious mind, you impress them upon your subconscious mind and what does that do? That has to be expressed through the body because the body is the instrument of the mind. So the body moves into action and produces a result.

Here is what it looks like:

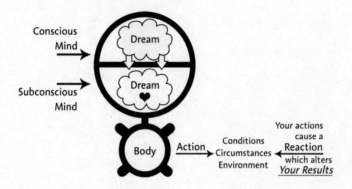

But then, you see, we go back to that old paradigm. We think, *What would they think? I mean, if some of the people I work with see me acting that way, they'll ask, "Who do you think you are?" And they'd start talking about me. I don't want them talking about me.*

You don't want them talking about you. I mean, what would you say? What are you going to say to your husband? Are you going to tell your wife? She's going to say, "Who are you trying to be? Grow up. Be yourself!" What you should say is, "That's what I am!" Because if you ever knew who self was—man, I'd shock you if I showed you self.

Can you see where this ridiculous conflict is going on inside?

# THE ONLY THING
# YOU CAN CONTROL

*Shifting from Reacting to Responding*

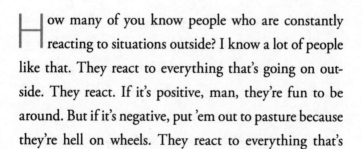

How many of you know people who are constantly reacting to situations outside? I know a lot of people like that. They react to everything that's going on outside. They react. If it's positive, man, they're fun to be around. But if it's negative, put 'em out to pasture because they're hell on wheels. They react to everything that's going on. They're not in charge of their life!

I was teaching some kids the difference between reacting and responding. I was talking to one little girl who was saying she got in trouble in school. I asked her why and she said because she hit one of the boys. I asked why and she said because "he's stupid."

I said, "Well, odds are pretty good that he's not going to get bright for quite a while . . . and you got in trouble for it."

She said, "Yes."

I said, "Why did you hit him?"

She said, "Because of the things he was saying."

I said, "I see. OK. Why don't you learn a new way to respond to these situations? You know, I have been around the park for quite a while and I have found that boys don't mature very fast, and some of them never do. But you're going to be around them and if you're going to react every time that they do something dumb, then you'll be going around in a reactionary state all the time. When a boy acts dumb, why don't you just say to yourself, 'Well, that was sure dumb of him. I'm glad I'm not like that.' Then go about your business. You wouldn't have gotten in trouble because you're not going to change his behavior anyway."

When you react, you put the situation or the person in control of you. When you respond, you stay in control. That's the difference between reacting and responding. That's not a big deal to learn, but I'm telling you that when you learn it, it is a big deal.

Now let's look at the graphic again:

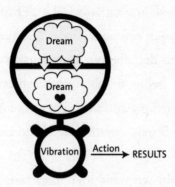

There's the conscious mind. All right. The conscious mind builds pictures. You think. You take those pictures. They're your dreams. And you impress those dreams upon the subconscious mind. So the picture you hold, you impress upon your subconscious mind. That idea is then expressed through the body into action. The action sets up a reaction. See, the Law of Attraction is actually the universe reacting to the energy that you're in. And the action/reaction alters the conditions, circumstances and environment, or in the vernacular, what we call the results.

That's the process. Let's go back over it again. You build the picture in the conscious mind. This is where you build your dream. You take that dream and you get emotionally involved with it. You *let* yourself get emotionally involved. You actually feel it all happening. That will change your emotional state. "Feeling" is a word we invented to describe our conscious awareness of vibration. That feeling or vibration is expressed in action. The action sets up a reaction. The action/reaction then alters our conditions, circumstances and environment in our life.

So what do we want to understand? We want to understand that our results (the conditions, circumstances and environment) are caused by what's going on in our mind. The reaction is actually the attraction.

It's a pretty simple concept. Would you agree? That's how it works. Who's got questions on this?

STUDENT: The things we say about spirit and thinking—the problem I have now is putting it to action. I know there is a spirit, but I don't know how to make the action happen. When you're talking sometimes I don't believe it, but I think, *OK, Bob has enough experience, I'm sure it's true!* And that's one thing. Then the other thing is about the Law of Giving—really, I am here right now, it might be selfish—but I want to get rich myself. I'm not thinking about getting money to give at this point. I want to get money myself.

BOB: Why do you want it?

STUDENT: I want to enjoy it.

BOB: How are you going to enjoy it?

STUDENT: The lifestyle. My family.

BOB: Now wait a minute. It's for your family. What are you going to do with the money? Are you going to give it to your family? Let's stay with this for a moment. Let's suppose you earn all kinds of money and you just keep it in your room in a drawer and every now and then you go and count it. You don't share anything with the family—"No, get out of here! I'm not going to give it to you!"—You'd be a miserable old man pretty soon, wouldn't you?

STUDENT: Well, we could buy houses . . .

BOB: You want to save some of these things and share it with them.

STUDENT: Sure.

BOB: You won't enjoy it until you do. If you get a new car, you don't really enjoy the car until you show it to somebody. You share the beauty or the comfort of the car with somebody and they'll say, "Gosh, this is really nice." You don't enjoy anything until you share it. I don't care if it's a sunset. You could be sitting there saying, "Wow, look at that. Isn't that beautiful!" But if there's somebody else there and you say, "Look at that! Wow! Look at that!!," you enjoy it more, don't you?

You should willingly give and graciously receive. It's a matter of keeping things moving. Keep it in the cycle. Circulation.

STUDENT: But I feel I don't have enough money to give now.

BOB: Give what you've got.

STUDENT [*laughing*]: But that's not my goal now. My goal is to *get* money.

BOB: I understand exactly where you're coming from and as we get involved in this I think you're going to get the answer to that. You will. Do you want to know something? There are a whole lot of people here in exactly the same spot, thinking *I'll give it if I get it, but I want to get it!* You are not on your own. We'll show you. You'll see.

**BOB:** Anybody else have a question on this? Yes.

**STUDENT:** In your model, we react because there is some action. And then you said that we were attracted to that action. Can you explain that further?

**BOB:** You've got to come to grips with this in your mind. You've got to act or respond in a controlled way—a way that attracts what you want instead of what you don't want. When you react, you are attracting what you don't want. In other words, you want to respond instead of react and then what you want will come back.

**STUDENT:** Why do so many people react?

**BOB:** We react because we've been trained to react. We let what's going on outside of us control of us. If we could stop and observe what's going on around us and stop reacting to it, we would be way further ahead. So I think that what happens when we change is we start to do that. We start to observe and not react and when we find ourselves going to react, we stop. We've got to first become aware of what we're doing. We don't change it right away.

I'll give you a good example of changing what's going on. When I was a little kid, I'd say, "Are yous coming?" If there was more than one it would be "Are yous coming?" That was very natural to me. It's more than one so it's *yous*, not *you*. There are three, four or five of you! Mrs. Gregory was my buddy Jack's mother. We used to be around their house and Mrs. Gregory would always say, "Bob, it's not 'yous,' it's 'you.'" So I thought, *She's really dumb. There's more than one, how could it be "you"?* She did not let up. Every time—"Bob, it's not 'yous,' it's 'you.'" She kept it up and kept it up. Then I got to a point where I'd say "Are yous coming?" and I'd be aware I said it. I could hear myself saying it. Then I got to the point where I'd stop when I was going to say "Are yous coming?" and I'd say "Are you coming?" It felt very uncomfortable. And now whenever I hear anybody say "Are yous coming?" I see Mrs. Gregory!

You first have to become aware of what you're doing. You have to become aware that you're reacting to situations. Then you have to stop yourself. Something inside wants you to react. You're going to strike back. You're going to react. You've got to stop yourself from reacting and take control of the situation. Sometimes there will be no reaction on your part at all. You will not do anything. You will take no action. You just observe and let it go. This is not an easy thing to learn. But I'm going to tell you—the compensation for learning it is astronomical. It is really good.

# THINK YOUR DREAMS INTO REALITY

*Thinking Your Dreams into Being*

I used to mentor a man who had more money than anyone I know. He had a 120-foot yacht that he would sail in the Caribbean, and then he would ship the yacht to the Mediterranean and sail in the Mediterranean. He had a beautiful place in Cap d'Antibes in the south of France. He had another place in Gstaad. He had a beautiful place in Eaton Square in London. If I took you in there and told you it was Prince Charles's condo, you would have believed me. This man was very wealthy and used to fly me down to his yacht in the Mediterranean or the Caribbean or maybe over to Cap d'Antibes. I would work with him for three or four days, for many thousands of dollars, and my job was to get him to go back to work.

That's right . . . he wouldn't work! I guess he wouldn't work because he was raised to believe that you worked to earn money, which he had more than enough of. That's a foolish idea, by the way, the idea that the end goal of work is to earn money. That's actually the worst way to earn money. But at any rate, I did my job, I did get him to go to work, and when I did, I was out of work. I enjoyed working with him.

One thing that really struck me about this client is the fact that he would play Louis Armstrong's song "What a Wonderful World" every morning. *Every* morning we could hear it throughout the vessel, throughout the place, wherever we were. It would play over and over and over again, and I thought, *You know, there's something to that!*

I suggest you put that song on an iPod or something and wake up to it every morning. You might want to get "I Can See Clearly Now" by Johnny Nash and "Pretend" by Nat King Cole, too, while you're at it. You know how that one goes:

*Pretend you're happy when you're blue*
*It isn't very hard to do*
*And you'll find happiness without an end*
*Whenever you pretend*

If you play songs like that all the time, you're going to program your mind. At first, you'll just pretend. But pretty soon, you'll find happiness without end.

Here's why:

Refer back to the stick person graphic. You see the conscious mind, the subconscious and the body. Here's what we want to know—the conscious mind is the thinking mind. It is also the educated mind. This is the part of the mind that school really focuses on. This is where the intellect and all those intellectual factors I was talking about are resident—in the conscious mind.

The emotional mind is quite different from the conscious mind. For the psych majors, the conscious mind is inductive and deductive. In other words, the conscious mind has the ability to accept and reject but it also has the ability to just accept. OK. The subconscious is totally deductive. In other words, it has no ability to reject. The conscious mind has the ability to choose. As this power flows into your conscious mind, you can choose what to do with it. You can choose anything you want to think. You can think anything you want to think.

This is huge when you think about it. There's a power flowing through you. There are some things you think you have to do. There are some things you think you can't control. There is only one thing you can control—and that's *you*. You can't control anything else. You can control your perception of something else. You can control how you respond to it. But you're in control of you. You have the ability to choose. You have the ability to accept or reject any idea. You know what you hear on television— you can reject it all. You don't have to accept any of it. When they talk about the economy going down the tubes—reject it. Someone comes along and they point out, "Well, these are the facts and you've got to pay attention to them!" You *don't* have to pay attention. You can reject it. I don't have to pay attention to something that I do not want to pay attention to. God gave me the ability to choose. I'm going to choose to reject all that jazz.

When you reject it, you have the ability to originate a thought. If you could see a beautiful power, it's flowing into your consciousness. It's like a funnel. It's flowing to and through you. When it flows into you it has no form. It has no form. It's a pure, unadulterated, creative energy that's flowing into your conscious mind. You have the ability to choose. Whatever you choose, and you impress, your subconscious mind must accept. It has absolutely no ability to reject. Your subconscious mind is totally deductive.

Now this is the part that you really want to try and grasp. Your subconscious mind cannot differentiate between what's real and what's imagined. If I put you in a hypnotic state, I could cause you to sweat. I could have you believing that it was 120 degrees in this room. And then a second later I could have you shivering because it's so cold. The temperature in the room didn't change, but your perception of the temperature in the room changed because of the idea I put in your mind.

I could turn my body as rigid as this table. It's called catalepsy. Because I tell it, it is stiff and rigid. Whatever I tell it to do. It's my body. Your body is an instrument of the mind. When you build an image in your mind of what you want, you've got to understand that your subconscious mind cannot reject it. It is totally subjective. One hundred percent. And it cannot differentiate between what's real and what's imagined. It must accept it.

What I just covered there—it's the most important thing you could ever learn.

Here's you and me today. There's a power. It's flowing

into your consciousness. You've got the newspaper . . . the radio . . . the TV . . . you name it. They're all flowing into our conscious mind. Because we have a reasoning factor—remember we said that reason was one of the intellectual factors—that's what gives us the ability to think. We can say, "I'm not going to accept that. I'm not going to think that. I'm not going to listen to that." We can just say I'm rejecting it and you could get rid of it.

But we don't do that. What do we do? I'll tell you exactly what we do. We leave our mind wide open when that stuff comes along. We don't even reason with it. We leave our mind wide open and it goes directly to our subconscious mind. Why do we do that? Because we're programmed to do it. That's where our paradigm is.

Hold your hand for a moment like this—put it on your chin for a second, would you do that? Come on. Where's your chin? What are you doing up there (*puts hand on cheek*)? Why'd you go there? Because I did. If I walked off a cliff, would you follow me? Come on!! Follow me!! You know what was happening? You weren't thinking! Your subconscious mind was wide open! You did exactly what I did!

That's the way we live. We see all those people out there and we're just following like sheep . . . "That must be the way to go! They're all going that way!!" No, that's really not the way to go! There's no business there. All the business is down here. See. You see two or three people going down and getting all the business. Why do we do that? That is what you have been raised to do! It's like speaking the language you speak. It's like liking the food you like. Why do you like it? You didn't decide you like the food. You say, "Oh, I decided." No, you didn't. Why do you speak the language you speak? You were trained to speak the language.

As an infant, your subconscious mind is wide open. Whatever is going on around you goes right into your subconscious mind. I want you to think of this for a moment. We can take a baby in any part of the world and before that baby is four or five years old—before she even goes to school, that baby could learn five languages, speak five languages fluently. That's not uncommon in some parts of the world. I had an associate in Kuala Lumpur whose little boy at four years old could speak four languages. Nobody thought anything of it. There were people around who were speaking four languages. The little boy spoke four languages. Here, I'm still learning one.

Do you know that you can teach a baby to read before the baby can talk, and then when the baby can talk you can give him a book and he'll read it to you? Remember, the subconscious mind will accept whatever you give to it. It's wide open.

Well, if you go into a welfare area, almost all welfare recipients are third-, fourth-, fifth-generation welfare recipients. Did your mother love you? So we go back through all that crap. Let's suppose we find the problem. You still have the problem! Why would you spend all that time looking for the problem? When you find it, you still have it! That's a form of psychoanalysis I think, isn't it? Let's throw that out. Let's just say that's part of the past. How about psychotherapy? That would be a little bit more progressive. Does that make sense?

OK. So, how do we get all of those ideas? Well, over and over and over that information is programmed into the subconscious mind. Look at this for a moment. The baby's mind is wide open. She will accept whatever you give to it. That's the language the baby learns. The baby's self-image is built at a very early age—before the baby even has the ability to think, before the conscious faculties have even been formed. This child cannot even think and yet the baby is building a self-image—what the baby thinks of herself. The truth is this . . . the baby is having the self-image built for her and more often than not, the person building it is ignorant about human potential. You find a child who's raised with a lot of praise and that child's going to grow up very confident. You find a child who's raised with a lot of criticism, he's going to grow up very insecure. You can put whatever you want into the baby's mind. Put it in over and over and over.

Why do you like the food you like? You were programmed to like it. Why do you speak the language? You were programmed to speak it. Why do you have the prejudices you have? You were programmed to have them. Why does one race of people think they're superior to all others? We're different colors, different shapes, different sizes and different genders. You know something—there's one common denominator—there's one mind. We are all an expression of exactly the same thing.

Oh, now all this conditioning—that conditioning turns into what is self-image, but self-image is only one idea. What were you surrounded by? Look at this for a minute.

Robert Heinlein was a science fiction writer in the 1960s. He wrote about a *Stranger in a Strange Land*, which is true, "In the absence of clearly defined goals, we become strangely loyal to performing daily trivia until ultimately we become enslaved by it."

This is true about most people. They become enslaved by trivia. That's all they know! Trivia! Nothing. There's not a creative thought that comes out of them in years. And they wonder why they're not enjoying life. What happened? Life's passed me by. What do you mean life's passed you by?

Well, if you're surrounded by people whose lives are filled with daily trivia, odds are pretty good that your life is, too. If you had people around while you were growing up believing that it was difficult to earn money, odds are pretty good you believe that, too. If you were surrounded by people when you were growing up who struggled just to make ends meet, they're good people, they just don't have much, but they're good. If you grew up around people who thought there's something wrong with having money, rich people aren't happy, I know rich people who laugh. Why did we grow up with these ideas? We grew up with all the prejudices and all the screwed-up thinking of the people we're surrounded by.

You say, "But I love my parents." Well, I love mine too but they didn't really have it very well put together. My father . . . I never really knew him. He was sort of a loser who left early. My mother was a beautiful person, a hard-working woman, but worked hard all her life. See. What were we programmed to do?

Let's just change the thinking. Let's reprogram the mind.

# YOU DON'T NEED TO DO IT ALL

*The Power of a Mastermind*

There's a story about my wife, Linda, that I was telling the consultants the other day. She rented a two-thousand-square-foot space and we met with a man from Today's Business who I was doing seminars for; they furnish offices. They dress 'em up, you know, do a real nice job. She hired them to come in and do her office. They had the right kind of furniture and carpets. Everything! So she got all these desks, all these . . . a lot of furniture, let's put it that way—two thousand square feet of furniture—and she started her own business. I said, "You've got to get people to start working with you!" Linda got people working but she was in far over her head.

I went home one day and found her in the bedroom under the covers. Literally, under the covers. She had them pulled up over her head. What do we do? We go back to the womb. Do you ever get like that? You get scared. You revert to the womb.

That's where she was. I said, "Linda, what's the matter?" She said, "I can't do this! I'm in over my head!"

What she wanted me to do is put my arm around her and say, "Honey, let me do it for you, I'll help you." Instead, I said, "Well then, *quit*!" And I walked out.

Do you know what happened? She straightened up under those covers and said, "You bastard—I'm not quitting." I thought, *It worked!* She didn't quit. She started to go.

You know, there's a little book I have: *As a Man Thinketh* by James Allen. I love this little book. He says: "A man only begins to be a man when he ceases to whine and revile, and commences to search for the hidden justice which regulates his life." A strong person cannot help a weaker person unless that weaker person really wants to be helped, and even then the weaker person must become strong himself. He must, by his own efforts, develop the strength that he admires in another. No one else can alter his condition.

See, I couldn't do it for Linda. She had to change her way of thinking, stop reacting to the circumstances and begin to use them to discover the hidden power and possibilities within herself. She had to do it for herself so she could grow.

Back in 1961 I was sitting and trying to figure out how I could earn the $25,000 I had written on my card. Then Ray showed me Step 6 in *Think and Grow Rich*. It's called "Organized Planning." Right at the top of a page it says, "Before you can be sure of your ability to transmute desire into its monetary equivalent, you will require specialized knowledge of the service, merchandise, or profession that you intend to offer in return for fortune."

You've got to have specialized knowledge if you're going to earn the money. And I didn't have any specialized knowledge. I didn't go to school. I didn't have any business experience. Poor me. I'm putting myself down, you know. I'm thinking of everything I didn't have. Ray told me that until I stop putting myself down I was never going to get up. He told me to start thinking of all the things I had going for me and to really get that I didn't have to have the specialized knowledge.

Now let's look at this part—this is just further down on the same page. This is rather good. Hill said, "The accumulation of great fortunes calls for power and power is acquired through highly organized and intelligently directed specialized knowledge, but *that knowledge* [my emphasis] does not, necessarily, have to be in the possession of the [person] who accumulates the fortune."

This is the second time I am sharing information from Mr. Carnegie . . . it is so important. Andrew Carnegie was the wealthiest man in the world in 1908. He was a poor little Scottish boy who came to America with his parents. He made his money in the steel business. Remember, he said in another part of the book that he knew nothing about the marketing or manufacturing of steel, and furthermore, he had no inclination to learn. He got everything he needed through the aid of his mastermind group.

If you think you need it all, forget it. You don't need it all. I clearly learned that I don't need it all. There's all kinds of things that I don't know. I have surrounded myself with some absolutely incredible individuals. If you got to know the people in our company, you would be very impressed. We have the most phenomenal people who you'll ever meet. Gina Hayden is a genius in execution. Man, she can make stuff happen! I can go—it doesn't matter where I go in the world—and everything's ready for me. I can go to Kiev—seven different languages we were dealing with, all translated simultaneously in seven different booths in the back. Everything just falls in place like clockwork. When I get off the plane, there's a limo waiting there. I don't have to worry about anything. Gina makes everything happen. We had Sandy Gallagher come into the company. She is an absolute genius with money. I have never seen anyone who understands money like she does. She can look at a financial statement and see something that the average person will never see. Just a genius when it comes to money. Mykie Oyler here—she writes some copy. I'll say, "Where'd you get that?" She'll say, "I wrote it." She's good, really good. She writes some neat stuff. We've got some phenomenal people in the company. Absolutely incredible. Everywhere you go, you're going to find some phenomenal people. Arash Vossoughi heads up our sales force. He is tremendous. You attract great people when you continually work on you.

You need "highly organized and intelligently directed specialized knowledge." But here's the key to it—you don't have to have it. Now, watch. You can obtain the specialized knowledge, saving yourself years of time-consuming study and hardship. There are going to be people who will be able to help you. The whole idea is to put as much out there as you can. You just have to think of more ways to help people. You don't have to worry about what's going to happen to you. You will find that the universe will reward you in abundance. Just think of how you can help other people. That's all you have to think about.

You don't have to know how to do everything. I'm just very good at what I do, and I get others to do everything else.

Do you know what the definition of creativity is? No routine. It is the opposite of routine. Get out of a routine. And you can get people to help you.

A mastermind is something you give to, not take from. If we're all giving, it's that mastermind energy that adds to all of us. Let's say Mykie and I are in a mastermind . . . we add to it, but carefully. Mykie will say, "Let's add Michelle." So something's arranged and I spend time with Michelle. Then I come back to Mykie and say, "I don't think so." I don't have to tell her why. The energy wasn't there. Not on the same frequency. It doesn't mean anything is wrong. But maybe Michelle and I are on the same frequency so I say yes, and it's all three of us on the same frequency. We're all in harmony.

It's not a brainstorming session. A real mastermind is when everyone comes together and they're in harmony. Most people don't have a real mastermind. Mark Victor Hansen and I have a mastermind—we invite people from time to time. That's where the Million Dollar Forum came from. It's about what you can give. If you go with that attitude—to give—you'll be amazed by what you get out of it.

# IT'S YOUR MOVE

*The Power of Decision*

There is a single mental move you can make that, in a millisecond, will solve enormous problems for you. It has the potential to improve almost any personal or business situation you will ever encounter . . . and it could literally propel you down the path to incredible success. I'm talking about decision.

You know, in fifty-plus years in the same business, you learn something if you really want to make things fly. I have found that most people have difficulty with decisions. They look at a problem, they see all the possible solutions, but they don't zero in on one. Until you zero in on one and take action on it, nothing happens.

Here's typically what happens. We have a stream of thoughts moving through our mind and we pick something that we really like. And we say, "You know what? This is what I really want to happen." And we set a target to shoot at.

But here's the mistake that most people make. They say, "I'm going to do that as soon as . . . I find the money. I'm going to take that vacation . . . as soon as I find the money. I'm going to open another office . . . as soon as I find the money."

Do you know something? You're *never* going to find the money. You're always looking for what you think you need to get to where you want to go on the frequency of your thoughts. But it doesn't work that way. You're not going to find what you're looking for on that level. You've got to be courageous. You've got to step out and say, "I'm going to do this and I'm going to do it *now*."

Edmund Hillary didn't know how to get to the top of Mount Everest until he got there. The Wright brothers didn't know how to get into the air until they got there. The second you make the decision—*Bingo!*—you flip your brain onto a different frequency and the appropriate thoughts start rolling into your mind. *That's* how it works!

This is one of the most important lessons I've ever learned. It has helped me earn millions. And it will help you to do the same.

The world's most successful people are all able to make decisions. Decision makers go to the top and those who can't make decisions seem to go nowhere. Think about it. Decisions or the lack of them are responsible for the making or breaking of careers.

Individuals who have become proficient at making decisions, without being influenced by the decisions of others, are the same people whose annual incomes fall into the six- and seven-figure categories. The people who never develop the mental strength to make these vital moves are relegated to the lower income ranks for all of their careers, and more often than not, their lives become little more than a dull, boring existence.

Of course, it's not just your income that is affected by

decisions. Your whole life is affected. The health of your mind and body, the well-being of your family, your social life and the types of relationships you develop are all dependent upon your ability to make sound decisions.

You would think that anything as important as decision making would be taught in every school. But it's not. And to compound the problem, decision making is not only missing from the curriculum of almost all of our formal educational institutions, it has been left out of virtually all of the training and human resource development programs in our corporate training world.

At this point, you could be asking yourself, "How am I expected to develop this ability?" Well, I have the answer for you. You have got to do it on your own. The good news is you've already begun by thinking about and digesting the information that I am sharing with you right now. This is causing you to become more aware of the importance of making decisions.

Most of us have weak decision-making muscles . . . we don't even recognize what it means to make a real decision. We fail to realize the force that a truly congruent, committed decision makes.

Part of our problem is that we use the term "decision" so loosely that it has come to describe our wishes, not our commitments. Instead of making decisions, we state our preferences. The word "decide" comes from the Latin *decidere*—the roots *de-*, meaning "off," and *caedere*, meaning "to cut"—therefore, making a decision means cutting off from any other possibility. A *true decision*, then, means you are committed to achieving a result, and then cutting yourself off from any other possibility.

After making a true decision, especially a tough one, you will usually feel a tremendous burden has been lifted from your shoulders.

Committed decisions show up in two places: your calendar and your checkbook. No matter what you say you value, or even think your priorities are, you have only to look at last year's calendar and checkbook to see the decisions you have made about what you truly value.

For example, I am committed to growth, both professionally and personally. A review of my calendar always shows multiple continuing education courses, seminars and workshops in both my personal and professional life.

Take a look at your calendar to see what it says about your values.

# WORK FROM THE HIGHER TO THE LOWER

## *Leave Your Senses Out of It*

In this session, we're going to break down the first page of Raymond Holliwell's chapter on the Law of Success in his book *Working with the Law*. This is a phenomenal chapter that we can take some great lessons from.

For instance, Holliwell said, "God intended every individual to succeed. It is God's purpose that man should become great."

Isn't that wonderful? God intended that you and I would become great.

In another book, a man named Robert Russell said, and I am paraphrasing, there is no secret to becoming great. You become great by doing little things in a great way every day.

So you don't have to look for something really big. Start right where you are. Do your best at everything you do.

Holliwell goes on to say, "It is God's will that man should not only use, but enjoy, every good in the universe. The Law of God denies man nothing. Man is born to be rich."

I created a program years ago that was based on everything I had learned at the time. It was called You Were Born Rich because it's true—you were born rich. You have deep reservoirs of talent and ability within you. You're probably just a little short of money. But as Holliwell says here, "The powers inherent within you are inexhaustible."

I want you to think about that for a moment. You have powers that are inexhaustible! This is a law.

He said, "Each normal person is endowed with a complete set of faculties which, if properly developed and scientifically applied, will ensure success, ever-growing success."

The great Napoleon Hill said, "An educated [person] is not, necessarily, one who has an abundance of general or specialized knowledge. An educated [person] is one who has so developed the faculties of his mind that he may acquire anything he wants, or its equivalent, without violating the rights of others."

But we're not taught to develop those faculties. We're taught to live by our five senses. Do you know what that does? It programs us to live from the outside in. It programs us to live from the bottom up. What do I mean by that? I mean, we live from the physical up to the intellectual or the spiritual. You're letting the physical control the higher, but it doesn't work that way.

God works from the higher to the lower. Spirit always manifests from the higher to the lower, from the nonphysical to the physical. If you're going to live in harmony with the law, that's the way you're going to have to work. You're going to have to work from the thought to the thing, and not from the thing to the thought.

Now what do I mean by that? I mean, don't let your bank account dictate your financial status.

One of the things I ask people when they first come to work with me is what's the most you've ever earned in a year? I remember asking one of my old business partners that question. He said, "$100,000." He was pretty proud of it and that was pretty good money.

I said, "If you do exactly what I tell you, I'll show you how to change that into a monthly income." And do you know that within months he was earning that as a monthly income? That's what we do. We teach people how to turn their annual income into their monthly income by setting up multiple sources of income.

Earlier I mentioned that Holliwell said that each normal person has a complete set of faculties that will ensure greater and greater success when they're developed properly. We've talked about those faculties before so I won't go into any great detail about them now. But, remember, you have perception—that's the way you look at life, your will—that teaches you to concentrate, your memory. There's no such thing as a bad memory; you have perfect memory. You have reason—that's your ability to think—and you have intuition and imagination. These are all phenomenal mental tools. You can develop them to experience greater and greater success. You're going to have to use them if you're going to live from the inside out.

Holliwell goes on: "Every man contains within himself the capacity for endless development."

Endless development! I don't know about you, but that excites me. I've been working on this now for over fifty-five years and I know that I'm going to study for the next fifty-five years. I just want to keep getting better at it.

Next he says, "Advancement into all things is the Law's great purpose. By learning to work with the Law in promoting that aim, man may build himself into greater and greater success."

So you might say, "What is the win for me in really studying these laws?" Well, that's it! You're going to build yourself into a greater and greater success. Now, that's a phenomenal idea! You're going to earn more money. And it will just keep going. I went from earning $4,000 a year to earning millions. And it's easier. I don't work as hard.

Napoleon Hill said it takes no more energy to work for the big idea than it does for the small one. Well, that's what we're saying here.

What else can you expect? Well, you're going to have more friends—better friends. You're going to live in a healthier body. You're going to enjoy your work more. You're going to do what you want to do. Live the way that you want to live.

Now listen to this. Holliwell said, "All the processes

of Nature are successful. Nature knows no failures." That's huge!

He continues: "She never plans anything but success. She aims at results in every form and manner. To succeed in the best and fullest sense of the term we must, with Nature as our model, copy her methods. In her principles and laws we shall discover all the secrets of success."

Isn't that exciting? We succeed when we model nature. I know one thing. The tide always goes out and the tide always comes in. The night always follows the day. Winter never follows winter. This is the law at work. It's perfect in all of nature. And we can do the same thing.

Next, he said, "In her principles and laws we shall discover all the secrets of success. Infinite resources are at man's disposal. There are no limits to his possibilities."

Think about it. Infinite. That means there are no limits on our ability.

And then: "He focuses and individualizes the elements, forces, and principles of the whole world."

The whole world! That's a bit of a stretch, isn't it?

Do you know that everything in this universe will rush to your aid when you are working in harmony with the law? This isn't some decision by some emotional or capricious God sitting on a cloud. This is the absolute law of the universe. The law is the uniform and orderly method of the omnipotent God. It's the way everything works. And everything works perfectly.

Holliwell continues: "He can develop a wonderful intelligence; thus, all life's questions may be answered, all Nature's secrets discovered, and all human problems solved. Nothing is impossible."

Now you may be thinking that the world is in dire need of this. Oh, you are so right!

But do you know it's because we're living in harmony with the law that we can live the way we do? Do you know there are some people who have never seen a toilet? Do you know there are some people who have never seen an electric stove? Do you know that the whole world lived like that not long ago? Do you know that the electric light is a brand new idea relative to most people in the world? Do you know that everything we've got that we take for granted is relatively new?

All of this happened just in the last century or so. Think about it. And it has happened because we started to understand the law. Think of what you can do when *you* understand the law.

Holliwell said:

*Higher faculties, remarkable talents, superior insight, and greater power are dormant in all, and by special psychological methods, these exceptional elements can be developed to an extraordinary degree for actual and practical use. Every mind can develop greatness. It is simply a matter of KNOWING HOW. True self-help, self-discovery, self-knowledge, and the proper instructions in applying one's faculties and using one's forces will advance any person.*

You see, the mind is perfect. It is perfect and man is not. We can think and our thoughts turn into things.
Holliwell said:

*Practice will ensure efficiency; use will bring forth results. Success, therefore, is within the reach of every aspiring man. Do you wish to succeed? You can. You possess all the essentials within yourself; all you need is to gain a right understanding of the principles and laws upon which success is based, and then to apply the right methods of operating these causes until success is earned.*

But you must earn it. There is no free lunch.

I've just touched on the first page of the Law of Success. As you get into this, you're going to realize that there's great help everywhere around us. We can have everything we want. We can enjoy all the good we want to enjoy. But only if we work in harmony with the law.

I started earning over a million dollars when I started cleaning offices. But you know, I think cleaning the offices was almost incidental to what I was doing. I could have been doing anything.

I had to find out what happened to me. Why did I change? Why did I go from being a loser to earning more than a million dollars?

What I really did was I changed my belief about who I am. I had read all of the religious books; I have a phenomenal library of religious and self-help books. I have over three thousand books in my personal library alone. But it wasn't until I'd read *Think and Grow Rich* that everything started to change. I had given that book to other people but nothing happened.

So I started to study to figure out why I had changed.

It took me nine years and what I arrived at is that I had changed my belief about who I am.

Do you know that if you really analyze most of your beliefs, you'd find they have no foundation? We believe lies.

Now you say, "Well, I believe that." And yet, our behavior would indicate that we've never heard of it. That's because there's a missing link. It's not obvious. It's inside.

Your success doesn't come from what you do. It's how you do it—it's what's going on inside. It comes from living in harmony with the law. There's a big difference.

# IT'S NOT ABOUT THE MONEY

*Having the Freedom to*
*Do What You Want*

Everything we want is already here—it's simply a matter of getting it. It's a matter of becoming aware of its presence. The main thing is to keep the main thing the main thing. What is the main thing? The main thing is freedom.

I had a mentor named Bill Gove. Bill is gone now, but he said, "If I want to be free, I've got to be me. Not the me I think you think I should be. Not the me I think my wife thinks I should be. Not the me I think my kids think I should be. If I want to be free, I've got to be me. And, I better know who me is."

I don't know how much you know about yourself, but I know when I started to study this, I knew very little about me. I knew my name, my weight, my height, my gender, my address, my phone number . . . beyond that I didn't know very much.

Think about this for a moment. Time and money freedom. We want time and money freedom. Well, you will be amazed at how much free time you have when you never have to think about money. If you've got money problems, it consumes your time.

When I was in debt everyone used to phone me and ask, "Where's the money, where's the money?"

I said, "If I knew where the money was, you wouldn't have to phone me!"

I earned $4,000 a year and I owed $6,000. That's not a good position to be in. You see, I was actually hopeless because I would have had to take every cent I earned for eighteen months just to get out of debt. And I would have nothing to live on. I think there are a lot of people who live like I was living. It's not fun. It's not even living—it is existing.

So what do we mean by time and money freedom? We want to have enough time to do what we want to do when we want to do it. And we want to have the money to be able to afford it.

It used to be that if I went in a store, I would look at the price tag and leave. But I want to be able to walk in if I see something I want and the price tag be the last thing I look at. You look at most people when they go shopping and the first thing they look at is the price tag. They're not getting what they want at all. They're getting what they think they can afford. Little do they know they could buy the whole store. Somebody did. It's important that we get this straight.

Do you know that there's an infinite source of supply? All religion and all science have always taught that. This is not my idea. This is something I have become aware of. When you're dealing with infinite, you can never take more than your share. There is an abundance for everybody.

I remember Ray Stanford. He took out a wad of money—the man always had a lot of money and I never had any—and told me that money couldn't talk but it can hear. If you call it, it will come. I never forgot that. I was calling it but it didn't come. It came when I understood abundance. When I understood the spirit of opulence.

You see, you can never take more than your share. We're dealing with the infinite.

I want you to think about this for a moment. Our world is changing. It is changing so dramatically and so rapidly that it is almost ridiculous. You know, it wasn't too long ago that when I did a seminar I'd have a great big chalkboard. And I'd have a lot of damp cloths because you've got to clean the board. I'd need lots of dry cloths so I could keep working and I needed lots of chalk. Today, I have a little three-pound computer. I can make all of these pictures and I can touch a button and *vavoom!*, the pictures change.

This world is getting smaller; it's not getting bigger. We're only hours away from anywhere now. You can do business all over the world. I have businesses all over the world.

Last Thursday I was working in Dublin. This Thursday I am in Melbourne. It wasn't too long ago that it would have been the experience of a lifetime to do that.

Now you can knock it out in a week, plus do a whole lot of other things as well. This world really is getting smaller. The chip has changed our whole life.

In 1970—that's before some of you were even here—I was on a program in Chicago with Eric Hoffer, the author of a terrific little book called *The True Believer.* This book is a classic. Anyway, during this program, Hoffer said, "In times of change learners inherit the earth; while the learned find themselves beautifully equipped to deal with a world that no longer exists."

In times of change, the learners will inherit the earth. I took that to be metaphoric for you will be happy, healthy and prosperous. You see, in 1970 things were really changing, but by comparison with now, they weren't even warming up. Look at the speed we're moving at today.

In times of change, the learners will inherit the earth, while the learned find themselves beautifully equipped to deal with a world that no longer exists. See, school leaves us with the idea that there's such a thing as a learned or an educated person. Do you know there's no such thing as an educated person? I don't know who thought of it, but it isn't so. There's no such thing as a learned person. You're either learning or you're not.

Yet the people who get the degree, and think they

have arrived, are wondering what happened. This world is changing. If you want to keep going, you've got to keep studying. You've got to keep learning. It should be a part of your daily experience—the same as eating or taking a shower. It's got to be something we're doing all the time. If we do, we'll inherit the earth; we'll be happy, healthy and prosperous. By many people's standards, at my age a person is considered old, yet I have more energy than most people who are twenty-three. I earn all kinds of money; I have all kinds of fun; I have all kinds of wonderful friends all over the world. But that is because I just keep studying. If you stop studying, it all goes away. It's that simple.

The chip in our computers has changed the world. It has changed it like night and day. Now I know there are people in this room who have never studied the things we're talking about. You ought to thank God that you're here. You see, I happen to believe that you're always in the right place for the right reason at the right time. This is the most powerful stuff that you're ever going to lay your hands on. I've got license to brag about it because none of it is mine.

I like the way Bill Gates put it. He said, "One thing is clear: We don't have the option of turning away from the future. No one gets to vote on whether technology is going to change our lives."

This isn't a democratic process. This is the deal. And you're either a part of it or you're not. You see this deal is strictly between you and yourself. No one else is involved.

Your problems are *never* about anyone else. If you have a problem, the person you should have a consultation with is always available. That's a good thing to remember.

Now think about this. How many would agree that financial success has a lot to do with being in the right place at the right time? How many would agree with that?

Almost everyone agrees with that. Well, there's something that's missing here. You've got to be aware that you're in the right place at the right time. The opportunities are always coming at us. If we're not aware, we miss them. Your results are an expression of your level of awareness. If you were aware of how to earn more money, do you think that you would ever settle for earning less? Of course not!

Remember, every religion and all science teach us that

everything we've ever wanted is already here. That being true, why don't we have more than we have? Because we're not aware of it. If you expand your level of awareness, your whole life will change.

You may be wondering how to expand your level of awareness. You do it through effective education combined with professional coaching over a reasonable period of time.

⋄

One of the key concepts to creating wealth is to understand that money is not the goal. That's right, I said, money is not the goal.

Frequently, people will tell me that they want to make money. However, I know it is not money they are really after. It's the things that money can buy and the freedom of time to do what they really want. While you may think this is an insignificant difference, it is actually the reason so many people never become wealthy.

Most of us were taught throughout our childhood that the whole point of making money is to sock it away and build our nest egg. We think of this as a type of insurance against bad fortune, accidents or old age when we can no longer work. The wealthy know that money only works when it is in motion—not when it's sitting in a bank account. You must understand that wealth is an ongoing journey of growth and circulation, and if that circulation is stopped, then the flow of money will cease.

While it may seem that there are many roadblocks on your journey to wealth, the only real obstacle is what you believe, think and feel about money. Most of us were raised with the cliché "Seeing is believing," which is a skeptical and negative view of life. Still, we hear it throughout our life until it becomes a part of our thought process without even realizing it. Wealthy people understand that this cliché is exactly backward—you must believe in what you can achieve before you will see it happen in your life. Wealthy people know that "Believing is seeing." The only thing that separates a millionaire from you right now is a wealthy mind-set, and the foundation of that mind-set is belief.

Does this mean that the wealthy have some special skill or knowledge? No—but they do possess some key characteristics that help them become wealthy.

The first of these characteristics is a willingness to listen to their own heart. If you could become wealthy by listening to the masses, then the masses would be wealthy and they are not. It is a natural tendency to ask the opinions of those we love or respect. Unfortunately, we listen to their comments and biases without taking into account the results in their own lives. We make a decision to listen based on our emotional attachment rather than by looking at what they have achieved. How can anyone who has not accumulated wealth advise you on how to do it? They can't.

A second characteristic of the wealthy is the ability to act when opportunities present themselves. Opportunity is often imagined to be something that you can't miss or pass up. However, I know from personal experience that opportunity is often only a whisper that comes during some of the most trying times of life. If you read the life stories of very wealthy and successful people, you will frequently find they were fired from jobs, kicked out of school or dealt with significant personal tragedies that other people would view as devastating. Instead, they viewed the challenges as opportunities and prospered.

The wealthy also understand that wealth is an ongoing process. It is not a destination you arrive at one day and then stop. It is also rarely accomplished overnight—although it can occur in a short period of time. However, if you gain wealth before you have gained a wealthy mind-set, then you are in danger of losing that wealth forever. We have all heard of those who win the lottery only to be near penniless a few years later. Since they were never taught to think wealthy, they have very little chance of achieving wealth that lasts, and ultimately they lose what money they have.

Those with a wealthy mind-set do what they love—and make money at it. Often I see individuals who are seeking wealth like it's something outside that they have to search for. In reality, wealth exists within you. You have activities and hobbies that you love and you can make these into your business if you choose to. Those who are successful and create a great deal of wealth do so because they are doing something they love. The money follows and is just a logical result of them realizing their dream. Money is not the dream.

Whether you grow up in the worst circumstance or have every advantage, you have the exact same potential inside of you to create the life you want. No matter how many times you read or hear someone talk about how to become wealthy, your life will never change until you believe that it can—believing is seeing.

# COUNT YOUR BLESSINGS

*An Attitude of Gratitude*
*Changes Everything*

Make sure that you're grateful every day. I don't care what your situation is, there is something for you to be grateful for. There are people who are living on less than $50 a year, are sick, have lost their home. So for some, it might be just being grateful for each breath or the ability to feel the sun on their face. But for the general population, we have so much to be grateful for.

Expressing gratitude works like magic. I remember doing a seminar in Phoenix one day when Sandy Gallagher, my business partner, was going through a rough time in her life. I was leaving town and she asked if we could grab a cup of coffee before I flew out.

So we went to a coffee shop and she asked if I could give her two or three ideas to help her maintain a good attitude. I said sure and took a napkin that was on the table. I grabbed a pen and wrote on the top of the napkin: "Every morning think of ten things that you are grateful for." Then, I said, "When you get finished writing the ten things down, send love to three people who are bothering you."

Now most people have difficulty doing that. If someone is really bothering them, they send bad energy to that person. Don't do that, send love to them. The person who is bothering you has nothing to do with this. It's the vibration you're putting yourself in. You're putting yourself into a wonderful vibration by sending love to them.

The third thing I told Sandy to do was to be quiet for five minutes and ask for guidance for the day.

Well, Sandy was heading to Hawaii to spend some time with her sister and mother so she had them get involved with this three-pronged practice each morning: writing down ten things to be grateful for, sending love to three people who are bothering you, and sitting quietly for five minutes and asking for guidance for the day.

On the first morning, Sandy, her sister and her mother thought it was a little bit of a dumb idea, but they did it anyway. And today, each one of them will tell you it changed their lives.

Wallace Wattles dedicated an entire chapter to the topic of gratitude in *The Science of Getting Rich*. On the first page, he said, "The whole process of mental adjustment and atunement can be summed up in one word, gratitude."

Now, let's look at the term "mental adjustment." If we have challenges in our life that are dominating our thinking—a shortage of money, a business problem, a relationship problem—we will have a tendency to focus on the problem. And by doing that, we add energy to what? The problem! And then the problem grows.

Wallace Wattles is saying don't do that. Get into the process of mental adjustment. See what you want. Don't spend any time looking at what you don't want.

Wattles said, "The whole process of mental adjustment and atunement can be summed up in one word: gratitude. The atunement is getting in harmony with the law.

How could we put that into action? Well, let's look at it this way. When you seem to be overwhelmed with problems, just stop whatever you're doing and block all of that stuff out. Then, think about all of the things that you have to be grateful for. I know that's a pretty big order, but if you do it, everything will start to shift in an instant. Just like snapping your fingers. When you change the way you look at the problems, the problems will change.

Gratitude is a powerful process for shifting your energy and bringing more of what you want into your life. Be grateful for what you already have and you will attract more good things. If you just study this one word, "gratitude," every day for a month, I guarantee that your life will shift.

Wattles also said, "The grateful mind is constantly fixed upon the best; therefore, it tends to become the best; it takes the form or character of the best and will receive the best."

"Gratitude" is a beautiful word, but it's also one of the most misunderstood words in any language. You see, gratitude hooks you up with your source of supply. It literally puts you in harmony with your source of supply so that the good in everything will move toward you.

# IT'S TIME TO STRETCH

*Your Great Idea Whose Time Has Come*

You don't *get* energy. People say, "Where does she get all that energy?" Nobody gets energy. Everybody releases energy. It flows to and through us. *There's no shortage of energy.*

You'll see a person come home from work and say, "I just haven't got any energy." You know what their problem is? They're *bored*! They're bored. Boredom is the absence of a creative idea. They may have *never* given birth to a creative idea! They just sort of go through life in a lockstep-type fashion. Doing what everybody does.

It started when they were little kids—going out and being like the other little kids, which is the only thing they can't be like—and so they spend their whole life trying to be like the other little kids.

I've *always* got a *big idea*. I go after goals I have no idea how we'll reach. But I know we're going to—I *know* we're going to. And the fact that I don't know how to do it doesn't scare me. It turns me on.

I've always found that big ideas grow even bigger when they're discussed and mulled over in a relaxed setting that's completely separate from a conference room or boardroom. In fact, many of the best ideas I've created have come from sitting at my kitchen table, doodling and brainstorming and looking out the window. It happens right there in my kitchen.

Alfred Adler once said, "I am grateful for the idea that has used me." When you fall in love with an idea, you will be grateful for that idea because it will move you into action.

What ideas wind you up and make you want to move into action? If you're not sure, get quiet and visualize. Visualization is where everything starts. When you think about it, everything begins with a picture. And the Law of Transmutation tells us that energy is always moving into form. You and I have been given creative faculties unlike any other form of life so we have the ability to create the vision or the image in our mind.

Everything you see right now all started as an image in somebody's mind. We always see the genius in somebody else, but never in ourselves. You are creative, powerful, innovative and you have genius locked up within you just waiting to be unleashed. Don't go another day down the path of a life that isn't completely satisfying.

You say you have ideas flooding your mind every day. Wonderful! So now what?

Ideas are useless if you don't take action to make them happen. But if you do, one good idea could change your entire life. It can change the world!

How would you like to have had the idea for the computer that you work on, or Facebook or Twitter? Stop and think of what the people who created the smart phone earned. Wouldn't you just love to be on the receiving end of that?

Unfortunately, almost all ideas are stillborn. People think about them but they die inside the person's mind. Beautiful ideas. Ideas that could change the life of the person who is entertaining them. But they never see the light of day.

Why?

It's like I said earlier—it's the start that stops most people. But the thing that is sitting on your shoulders will create ideas. And everything around you is nothing but the expression of an idea.

You started out with a very beautiful imagination. But they got you in school and *Wham!*, they knocked it out of you. They called it not paying attention.

Well, let that go. Don't live there anymore. Andrew Carnegie, who was the wealthiest man in the world in the early 1900s, said he knew nothing about the manufacturing or the marketing of steel. And yet he became the wealthiest man in the world in the steel business.

Now how did he do that?

He did it with a team. No one in the history of the

world who has ever done anything of any consequence has ever done it on their own.

Stop letting your ideas die inside of you. Get help where you need it so they can be born. Dedicate your life to a worthy idea—an idea so big and exhilarating that you're grateful for the idea that has used you.

# AFTERWORD

One thing should be clear from even a casual perusal of Bob Proctor's lectures—he is not a typical motivational speaker. The truth is, Bob Proctor does not see himself as a motivational speaker. He teaches method living, much the same as Stella Adler taught method acting. He doesn't provide Band-Aids for the problems and challenges we face each day. And he doesn't address symptoms. He goes right to the cause of what's keeping us stuck so we can move on to a bigger life.

Bob Proctor has an exalted idea of life. He believes you shouldn't just be content, you should be joyful. Your body shouldn't just feel OK and be pain free, it should be vibrantly healthy and energetic. You shouldn't just be able to pay the bills and take a vacation once a year, you should have all the money you want to do everything you want to do.

Bob doesn't hope all of those things can happen, he *knows* they can happen and they *will* happen if you learn to do one thing: live in harmony with the laws of the universe.

Bob didn't come to this realization quickly or easily. It took decades of studying Napoleon Hill's *Think and Grow Rich*, years of working with his mentor Earl Nightingale and a voracious appetite to learn everything he can about universal laws. Bob has been studying and applying this material every day since 1961.

This is not a conventional "how-to" book because Bob is not a conventional man. In fact, he abhors conforming and being normal. He says we should never follow the masses because the masses don't know who they are, where they're going or what they really want.

Instead of providing a cookie-cutter equation for living a healthy, happy and wealthy life, the lessons in this book have a broader goal. The purpose of these classes is to raise your level of awareness of who you are and what is really possible for you when you live in harmony with universal laws. That's not something you can learn overnight, in a month or in a class. It's a lifelong journey. But know this: as you start to understand these laws and make a conscious effort to apply them, your life will just keep getting better and better every day.

—SANDRA GALLAGHER